MW01491573

A Blacklist Education

A Blacklist Education

American History, a Family Mystery,
and a Teacher Under Fire

Jane S. Smith

RUTGERS UNIVERSITY PRESS
NEW BRUNSWICK, CAMDEN, AND NEWARK, NEW JERSEY
LONDON AND OXFORD

Rutgers University Press is a department of Rutgers, The State University of New Jersey, one of the leading public research universities in the nation. By publishing worldwide, it furthers the University's mission of dedication to excellence in teaching, scholarship, research, and clinical care.

Library of Congress Cataloging-in-Publication Data

Names: Smith, Jane S. author
Title: A blacklist education : American history, a family mystery, and a teacher under fire / Jane S. Smith.
Description: New Brunswick : Rutgers University Press, 2025. | Includes bibliographical references and index.
Identifiers: LCCN 2024049508 | ISBN 9781978845053 cloth | ISBN 9781978845077 epub
Subjects: LCSH: Public schools—New York (State)—New York—History—20th century | Blacklisting of teachers—New York (State)—New York—History—20th century | Anti-communist movements—New York (State)—New York—History—20th century | New York (N.Y.). Board of Education—History—20th century | Education and state—New York (State)—New York—History—20th century | Schur, Saul, 1911–1988 | McCarthy, Joseph, 1908–1957—Influence | Teachers—New York (State)—New York—Biography | LCGFT: Biographies
Classification: LCC LA339.N5 S65 2025
LC record available at https://lccn.loc.gov/2024049508

A British Cataloging-in-Publication record for this book is available from the British Library.

References to internet websites (URLs) were accurate at the time of writing. Neither the author nor Rutgers University Press is responsible for URLs that may have expired or changed since the manuscript was prepared.

♾ The paper used in this publication meets the requirements of the American National Standard for Information Sciences—Permanence of Paper for Printed Library Materials, ANSI Z39.48-1992.

rutgersuniversitypress.org

To the memory of Saul and Sylvia, the first teachers

Contents

A Blacklist Education

Introduction

The year I entered kindergarten, my father got kicked out of school. It took many years for me to learn that he had been the victim of an almost-forgotten campaign to purge liberal and left-leaning teachers from the public schools. When I decided to uncover what had happened to him, I had little idea how much of twentieth-century history would be involved.

This is the story of a double education. For my father, Saul Schur, it was an education into the challenges of being an active citizen and a public employee in the 1950s, a time of blacklists, loyalty oaths, banned books, and forbidden topics. Harassed and investigated for what he considered good deeds, he learned the hard realities of repressive politics. He was taken down as brutally as any victim of school-yard bullies.

For me, uncovering the teacher blacklists was an education in sympathy and outrage. I learned that the man I had known as a genial skeptic, open to progressive causes but not at all optimistic of their success, had once been a passionate activist and a thorn in the side of his superiors. As I realized how little I had known about Saul's life as a teacher, I also gained a much broader understanding of the disputed and often resentful attitudes toward teaching in a country forever struggling with the meaning of democracy.

My clearest memories of early childhood date from the months when my father was being investigated and I was just entering public school. Finding out about his struggles helped me make sense of what had been a scattering of brightly colored little mysteries—including the puzzle of why the events of one early year, when I was just on the cusp of retained memory, are so much more vivid than those from later periods of childhood.

But first, there was just a chaotic jumble of family papers. After my mother, Sylvia Schur, died at the age of ninety-two, following several stupendously disorganized moves, I had the daunting task of clearing out her files. Amid cabinets full of expired insurance policies, ancient travel brochures, outdated business correspondence, and holiday greetings from earlier decades, I found a large accordion file stuffed with photographs, newspaper clippings, and miscellaneous documents relating to my father, who had died over twenty years earlier.

It was a strange assortment. Letters from Eleanor Roosevelt, Hollywood producer Cecil B. DeMille, and the New York City Board of Education. Glossy black-and-white photographs showing my father on a picket line and as a participant in earnest gatherings intent on unidentified projects. A newspaper clipping about a testimonial banquet in his honor attended by high-ranking New York City politicians. A wallet-size card attesting that my father—a man who suffered from hay fever, seasickness, mechanical ineptitude, and a general indifference to team activities—had been a Boy Scout troop leader.

All of this was complete news to me. Nothing in the file was dated later than 1953, although my father lived another thirty-five years. Little seemed related to the affable and bookish man I knew.

Shortly after I came upon this collection, I happened to read a newspaper feature that sent me tumbling down one of the bumpier rabbit holes of American history. The article was about teachers blacklisted by the New York City public schools in the 1950s. I knew my father had been a high school English teacher in the early 1950s and that the school where he taught had been racked by conflict. I had heard him mutter, from time to time, about evil people who had risen to power in the city schools. He had always said he left teaching voluntarily. Now I wondered if there was more to the story. Following a clue in the article, I wrote to the New York City Municipal Archives and asked if my father was one of the blacklisted teachers described in the feature.

Yes, the archivist in charge of the Board of Education anticommunist collection answered. Would I like a copy of his file?

This was not a simple question. All parents are a puzzle that their children spend a lifetime trying to solve. Sometimes you find secrets you wish had stayed hidden. Sometimes, though, you are handed a piece of information that rearranges the past into a clearer pattern you hadn't even known existed. I wanted to know what had been happening in my family.

A few weeks after I sent my proof of relationship and a check for nineteen dollars to cover photocopying, I received a package that included a redacted transcript of a very bizarre interrogation. People code-named "Falcon" and "Sugar" said my father was a communist, or had been a communist, or had associated with people who were or had been communists. How did they know? No evidence seemed necessary for these vague assertions, which, as I discovered, often cited groups that do not exist in any other record.

As I worked to identify the contents of the mysterious accordion file and put them into their historical context, I came to recognize that being investigated for allegedly subversive activities, so pivotal an event in my father's life, was a depressingly ordinary moment in the twentieth-century annals of political intimidation. Many people are aware of the Red Scare of the 1950s. Senator Joseph McCarthy, whose name is often used as shorthand for an entire era, was ruining lives by insisting that dangerous communist zealots had infiltrated federal offices, newspapers, labor unions, and the armed forces, working to undermine the United States and all it stood for. McCarthy was unable to prove even a single claim, but the mere accusation of disloyalty gave him enormous power to get people fired or imprisoned, particularly since he was supported by FBI director J. Edgar Hoover. Separately, but very much in collaboration, the Senate Internal Security Subcommittee conducted hearings on what it claimed was a pervasive threat of espionage in the United States. In the House of Representatives, the House Un-American Activities Committee, better known as HUAC, subjected intellectuals, artists, writers, and performers to similar inquisitions, both in Washington and in other cities around the country. These were very public spectacles, particularly when Hollywood stars were in the witness chair. They have been studied and reenacted many times in print, on stage, and on the screen.

What is almost forgotten is that several state and local school systems, and notably that of New York City, the largest school system in the country, carried out parallel hunts for alleged subversives in the virulently anti-communist years after World War II. The special investigator appointed by New York City's Board of Education operated with far less publicity than the red-hunting members of Congress, but for the teachers involved, and for the future of public education, the impact was just as great. For my father's generation, raised to revere the power of education and the promise of democratic equality, the new reality of political persecution brought a deep sense of betrayal. Like many others, Saul did not just lose his job. He was robbed of his ideals.

The most damning accusation in my new transcript was that my father had been a member of the Teachers Union, once the major labor organization representing public school teachers in New York City. Like my father, you might think it was acceptable or even laudable to be active in a labor union while working at Samuel Gompers Vocational High School, named for the founding president of the venerable American Federation of Labor. Like my father, you would be wrong. He had joined the Teachers Union in the 1930s, when it offered unique support for the thousands of New York City teachers consigned to part-time positions. There were communists in the Teachers Union, a fact that had become damning during the aggressive anti-communist investigations of the 1950s. The new rules of guilt by association meant that my father must be a communist, too, and therefore automatically classed as a danger to his students and to the country he loved.

The goals of the Communist Party USA in the 1930s were higher wages, full employment, wide access to housing and education, recognition of unions, and an end to racial and religious discrimination. I am sure my father shared these goals. Still, I can find no evidence of actual Communist Party involvement or reports of political advocacy in his classes. All I have are the unreliable, unsubstantiated, and often coerced recollections by unidentified informers that were the grounds for his investigation.

To clear his name, Saul needed to present evidence that he was no longer a communist, which is as loaded a query as the famous no-win question, "Have you stopped beating your wife?" Alternately, by the peculiar rules of American anti-communist investigations of the 1940s and 1950s, he could prove his loyalty to the United States of America and his obedience to the New York City superintendent of schools by providing the names of anyone who might have ever attended meetings of organizations that had subsequently been judged to be subversive. Even the most casual association, decades ago, was considered evidence of current, dangerous disloyalty.

New York City was not the only site of school purges. In California, campuses at the state universities were roiled by the sudden demand that faculty members sign a loyalty oath. Several of the most prominent professors left for other universities, while others agonized over how they would support their families if they were suddenly without a job. Public school teachers in Connecticut, Massachusetts, Pennsylvania, Colorado, and other states lost their jobs, often because of the flimsiest accusations. But New York was the largest city and the one with the most diverse population of both students and teachers, and its purge was the biggest.

Between 1949 and 1954, almost a thousand New York City teachers were targeted for special inquiries by the city's Board of Education, often because of uncorroborated reports from paid informers or anonymous accusers. Professors at the city's public colleges and universities were also investigated by the separate Board of Higher Education, but it was in the elementary and secondary schools that accusations were most doggedly pursued. Investigators questioned teachers at their homes, accosted them in their classrooms, and ordered them to report for individual hearings held in a secret chamber at a Board of Education storage building in Brooklyn.

Unlike the more famous House and Senate hearings, these interrogations were not published, filmed, open to the public, or reported in the news. No lawyers were allowed, although the interrogator was himself a lawyer. A stenographer took notes, and people working with the investigators could watch through a two-way mirror to detect what were construed as guilty expressions or gestures.

Teachers who didn't appear for their interview were fired for "insubordination," a charge that saved the Board of Education the burden of proving any actual wrongdoing. The same fate awaited teachers who refused to discuss their political views, saying the questions violated their constitutional rights. They, too, were fired for insubordination.

Those under attack were not allowed to know who accused them or what crimes (beyond "insubordination" or "conduct unbecoming a teacher") they supposedly had committed. The only way to save their jobs was to name other teachers as subversives. Again, no proof need be provided. Indeed, a state statute passed in March 1951 specifically suspended the rules of evidence for such inquiries. Any objection to answering questions about past or present political sympathies, including invoking the Fifth Amendment right against self-incrimination, was considered an admission of guilt.

The New York City teachers' crimes, whatever they were, had nothing to do with classroom activities. Excellence in teaching was irrelevant or, worse, a reason for suspicion. An effective teacher was especially dangerous, "like Socrates," one of the prosecutors for the Board of Education remarked, citing the famous fifth-century-BCE teacher sentenced to death for corrupting the minds of the youth of Athens with his heretical ideas.

A few teachers took to the courts. Others yielded to pressure and turned informer themselves, reporting or fabricating scraps of long-past conversations overheard in offices, at parties, or even in restrooms— words that took on sinister meaning under the prodding of the investigators. At least one teacher committed suicide after being pulled from her kindergarten classroom for questioning.

By 1956, over three hundred New York City teachers had been fired or pressured into resigning. Others had been "allowed" to retire early. The lawsuit filed by nine of the first teachers brought in for interrogation, *Adler v. Board of Education*, went all the way to the U.S. Supreme Court, where a 6–3 decision in 1952 ruled that "appellates were not deprived of free speech, but merely of the privilege of public employment." In his dissent, Justice William O. Douglas warned that the New York law fostered "guilt by association" and turned schools, "the cradle of our democracy," into "a spying project" and "a police state" that denied teachers freedom of thought and expression. It took almost twenty years for a different Supreme Court to reverse the decision. The teachers in the case won reinstatement and pensions, though they received no compensation for their years of unemployment.

Those were the stubborn, litigious few. Most of the targeted teachers resigned or retired without any public process, their names recorded only in obscure municipal files and their futures never known. The teachers who lost their jobs in New York City and other areas were not famous or important, except as their ordeals remind us of a time when repression was so very common. Their absence becomes the invisible outline of an educational void, a narrowing of thought that pervaded classrooms for many years.

My father was one of hundreds of these forgotten teachers whose lives were upended by the anti-communist investigations. He did his job with all the usual triumphs and failures of what, in another place or time, would have been an entirely unremarkable career as a high school English teacher. As it happened, though, he taught at a school that careened from crisis to crisis in an era when problems rooted in greed and fear were magnified by much larger national conflicts of class, religion, and political ideology.

Like most of the blacklisted teachers, Saul was not a radical intent on overthrowing the U.S. government. He was an advocate for better classrooms for children and improved working conditions for teachers, a supporter of racial and religious freedom, an enemy of corruption, a believer in standing up and being counted, and perhaps a bit of a political naïf. Most of all, he was a product of changing times, molded by a progressive educational system that dedicated itself to filling his head with what he was told were the most prized national virtues—justice, fairness, equality, and civic engagement—and then, under different leaders with different values, attacked him for taking those virtues seriously.

Was he also, ever, a member of the Communist Party? It is possible. Many people were drawn to communism in the 1930s, when the failures of the American economy were visible all around them and the terrors of Stalinism were not yet known. In the depths of the Great Depression, New York City was awash with dreams of reforming the world, including the vision of an egalitarian collaborative utopia.

Saul attended City College, the nation's first tuition-free college and one that still serves the children of immigrants and the working class as a springboard to opportunity. In the early years of the Depression, students spent hours standing in the lunchroom arguing about the best way to rescue an economy that was clearly broken. Asking if Saul had ever associated with people who sympathized with communists, socialists, Trotskyists, Bolsheviks, or adherents to any of the other progressive ideological factions that proliferated in New York City, and especially at City College, was as meaningless as asking a graduate of Texas Tech if he had ever associated with people who followed football. Trained as a teacher and then unable to get a job for much of the 1930s, he certainly had enough free time to attend meetings and rallies, and more than enough reason to think society could be organized to treat workers more fairly.

As for specific activities or even socialist sympathies, the record is blank. Ours was not a house that rang with denunciations of capitalism or glorifications of worker solidarity. My brothers and I never went to any of the "red-diaper baby" summer camps outside New York City, like Kinderland in the Berkshire Mountains or WoChiCa (short for Workers Children's Camp) in rural New Jersey. We had a record player and a radio, and eventually a television, but I heard no songs of revolution or protest. My father's musical taste ran to opera, my mother's to silence. I am told we had a record of Paul Robeson in the house, but I never heard of him or other blacklisted performers like Pete Seeger until I got to high school during the folk revival of the 1960s.

My parents were part of that great American tradition of quick-change artists who enter the world among people who don't speak reliable English and exit with subscriptions to the *New Yorker* and a lifetime membership at the Museum of Modern Art. Like armchair liberals of a later generation, they demonstrated their progressive ideas mostly by going to foreign films and voting for Democrats. Decades later, when a family friend was boasting of her communist youth, my father laughed at her pretentions of a radical past. "Sure, you went to rallies," he said. "All the college girls did. That's where you met guys." Of course, that assumes college boys were also at the rallies, and it certainly seemed as if he was speaking from personal memory. Whether attending a rally makes you a collaborator with the hosting organization is, of course, a matter of opinion.

What I do know is that he was an active member of the Teachers Union, like thousands of other New York City teachers, and that the Teachers Union had avowed communists among its leaders. None of this was illegal, uncommon, or in any way illicit.

Until it was.

In 1954, after decades of fearmongering about the Red Menace, Congress unanimously passed the Communist Control Act, outlawing the Communist Party in the United States and potentially stripping citizenship from its members. Like so many events of the time, the Communist Control Act was a piece of political theater that allowed both conservative Republicans and liberal Democrats (like Senator Hubert Humphrey, one of its sponsors) to show they were "tough on Communism." Vaguely written, hastily enacted, frequently attacked in state courts and public forums as both unconstitutional and unenforceable, it has never been repealed.

The anti-communist frenzy of the 1940s and 1950s enabled mid-twentieth-century American political conservatives to reshape schools in an image that better reflected their own biases, controlling who could teach and which books could or could not be read. The effort to instill a narrow brand of conservative ideology was only partly successful, as shown by student activism of the 1960s and 1970s. But for almost two decades, people in power were in the business of repression and exclusion. Doubtless there are other versions of these events, and certainly there are more exhaustive histories of the anti-communist purges. Here is what I believe was going on.

Terrestrial Navigation

Whenever I find myself at an exhibit featuring New York City street photographers of the mid-twentieth century, I scan the walls for familiar faces. Maybe I'll catch a glimpse of my parents, my older brother, aunts, uncles, cousins, even the ghosts of the grandmothers who died before I was born but are still recognizable from family albums. They were all living there, after all: shopping, walking, passing through revolving doors, waiting for a traffic light to change, part of that vibrant community of strangers who made up the city.

I might also see a picture of my childhood self, because in the summer of 1952, when I was four years old and about to enter kindergarten, my father and I spent a lot of time walking the streets around our home in Lower Manhattan. My mother, a magazine editor, worked late hours and many weekends, darting in and out of my waking life in a flash of lipstick and pearls. To me, she was a glittering but very distant star. My brother, nine years old and already allowed to ride the subway by himself, was often out and about. When home, he spent what seemed like a great deal of time devising traps to catch me if I tried to enter his room or touch his collection of comic books. In my little galaxy, he was a forbidden planet.

My father and I, by contrast, were held by the gravitational pull of our immediate neighborhood, our rotation determined by a round of errands. Starting from our front door at Fourteenth Street and Avenue B, we went to the shoemaker, the dry cleaner, or the stationery store. The north side of the street was lined with the bland brick towers of Stuyvesant Town, the planned community of middle-income apartments

Saul and his youngest pupil, circa 1951. Credit: Collection of the author.

where we lived. The south side of Fourteenth Street, however, and everything below it, held a fascinating helter-skelter of walk-up tenements, small stores, street peddlers, and fragments of the city's historic past. We walked south to the public library on Tenth Street, where the children's room had huge arched windows that looked out on Tompkins Square Park. On the way to the library, we passed the looming brick mass of P.S. 61 on Tenth Street and Avenue B, where my older brother was entering fifth grade and where I would start kindergarten in September. Other days we walked east almost to the FDR Drive and the Con Ed electrical plant, two massive concrete expressions of modernity, or west to Union Square, where a bronze statue showed George Washington stretching his right arm forward as though to seize a piece of history as it passed. While we walked, my father introduced the basics of urban geography to a captive preschooler.

I learned to add and navigate at the same time, starting from the front door of our apartment building. As far as I knew, the whole world was laid out in rectangular blocks bounded by streets with easy-to-remember names. Going east to west, there were Avenues C, B, A, then First through Fifth, which was as far as I got. South to north was even simpler, as easy as counting by ones. The southern border of my personal map started at Seventh Street, the lower end of Tompkins Square Park, and continued north as high as I could count.

As we exited the elevator and stepped through the lobby to the sidewalk, my father might pose an arithmetic question.

If we walk two blocks north, where will we be?

Fourteenth, Fifteenth, Sixteenth Street! I would crow with triumph.

Good, he would say. *Now what if we go two blocks west?*

First Avenue!

I was small but clever, good with numbers.

Also, my father cheated. He never quizzed me south of Canal Street, never mentioned the confusing diagonals of Broadway or the Bowery. He was an experienced teacher and knew that early triumphs are a solid foundation on which to build extensive knowledge. Once a student had a grasp of the rules, the exceptions could follow.

I didn't know at the time that his instructional load had been reduced to a single pupil: me. In September, after fifteen years of teaching in the English Department at Samuel Gompers Vocational High School in the South Bronx, he would start at a new school, demoted to a temporary position in a job he strongly suspected would not last. He was already under investigation, caught in a cloudy web of accusations and insinuations that was as damning as it was nebulous.

While I was looking forward to kindergarten at P.S. 61, my father was struggling against nameless, faceless enemies whose charges, cloaked in the routine jargon of official procedures, sought to discredit everything he had ever done and jeopardize the only career he had ever wanted. There is an old joke that academic battles are so fierce because the stakes are so low. When it is your job and your identity that are threatened, however, the stakes seem very high. And so we walked, me learning about local landmarks and my father contemplating a very uncertain future.

Here are some other things that happened in the United States in the summer of 1952. Dwight Eisenhower won the Republican nomination for president and chose as his running mate Senator Richard Nixon, who had built his 1950 senate campaign on false accusations that his opponent had communist ties. Another Republican senator, Joseph McCarthy of Wisconsin, who liked to brandish (but never actually disclose) what he said was a list of communist subversives, campaigned for reelection to a seat he would easily win in November. Julius and Ethel Rosenberg, already convicted of espionage, mounted what would be an unsuccessful appeal of the death sentences that would lead to their electrocutions in 1953, the first executions for treason since the Civil War. And my entire family went to the hottest musical on Broadway, *The King and I*.

The show, loosely based on the memoir of a British governess in the royal court of Siam in the middle of the nineteenth century, was a very contemporary parable of political reform. According to *The King and I*, Anna, the governess, overturned a history of regal tyranny by deploying education, persuasion, persistence, and a very catchy polka. Along with "Shall We Dance?" (the polka), the show includes a musical version of "fake it 'til you make it" psychology called "I Whistle a Happy Tune." There are also several love songs, extravagantly exotic costumes, and enough tragedy to bring the audience to tears. And it was all about the power of a harassed and very dedicated teacher.

The King and I had already won Tony Awards for best musical, best actor, and best actress when we crowded into a giant Checker cab for the ride north to the theater district. My brother and I perched on the metal stools that folded down in the front of the roomy back seat where our parents sat with Saul's father and stepmother. Morris and Helena Schur were in town for a very rare visit from San Francisco, where they had moved from New York shortly after my parents married in 1938.

These grandparents were, to me, a fascinating departure from the loving, homespun elders I saw in picture books. Morris, always impeccably dressed, seemed to barely know I existed. Helena was a short, buxom, raven-haired sage who never appeared in public without high heels and full makeup. Her family had fled the Russian pogroms for

Guatemala, where she had grown up before moving to the United States, and her pronouncements in fractured Spanglish were the stuff of family legend. It was during this visit that she observed that the recently elected president of Guatemala, who favored land reform and a minimum wage, would not last in office. "It's impossible," she explained. "Nobody is for him but the people." My parents roared, though subsequent events showed Helena was right.

When we got to the St. James Theater, we were led to wonderful seats in the front of the orchestra. Everything about the show was thrilling. The king was bald and barefoot and spoke with an odd accent, but he was also handsome and a little scary. Anna was a very brave teacher who wore shimmering dresses with huge hoop skirts. While everyone else bowed before the king, she stood up to him. When she was afraid, she whistled a happy tune. When threatened, she taught the king to dance. His many children of various ages, also barefoot, performed in a play about escaping oppression called "The Small House of Uncle Thomas," which I assumed was original to the show I was watching. I was four years old. I was mesmerized.

Decades passed. One day when my father was visiting my family, I watched my own rambunctious four-year-old noisily zooming around the room with a plastic action figure in each fist, and suddenly the trip to *The King and I* popped into my mind. What had possessed him, I asked, to buy a child so young an expensive orchestra seat for a Broadway show? We were not theater people. We were not rich. This had been an unprecedented, never-repeated outing.

"Oh, that's easy," my father answered. "My folks were visiting from San Francisco, and I was about to lose my job. We wanted to show them we were solvent."

I had expected a story of lucky connections: somebody who knew somebody who had last-minute theater tickets. Instead, I realized, I had played my own supporting role in an exercise in brave deception, a version of whistling a happy tune. I regret to say I got distracted, probably by that same four-year-old, and so I didn't ask how my father lost his job. By the time I began to wonder, all the people who could tell me were long gone.

I should add that this theatrical extravagance, grand as it was, did not break the family budget. My mother was then the food editor of

Look, a glossy magazine of wide circulation and decent salaries—not decent enough that my father's paycheck was dispensable, but enough that we could afford such a one-time indulgence. Had she not been so gainfully employed, our lives would have been much more strained, not just after the blacklists but also before. Put another way, teaching was a luxury my father could afford without depriving his family. It was his passion, and he made sacrifices—in time, income, and persecution and official abuse—to follow his chosen career.

Morris and Helena returned to San Francisco a few days later, and my father and I resumed our walks. As the summer days grew shorter, we added the glowing skyline to our lessons in terrestrial navigation. The bright art deco fan of lights on top of the Chrysler Building, snapping into visibility at the first hint of dusk, was my North Star. The gilded beacon on the MetLife Tower, at Madison Avenue and Twenty-Fourth Street, was better than the sinking sun for steering me west. Giant neon signs across the water marked the East River, which any dodo knew meant east. Once you had the other three directions, south was easy.

There were other things to learn as we took our walks around Lower Manhattan. Watch the traffic lights and look both ways before crossing a street. Do not fall down an open manhole (something I had already done as a toddler, with a lifetime scar to prove it). Do not stand over subway grates, share a ball into traffic, or get within arm's reach of those disheveled men sprawled by the curb. Always know at least two ways to get home. Finding a new route could be just as important as tracing an old one, a lesson I absorbed long before I understood its many meanings.

It took me years of surprised confusion in places with fewer neatly numbered blocks to abandon my childish impression that I had an excellent sense of direction. For my father, the ground shifted more suddenly, and the dislocation was more extreme. All at once, it seemed, his professional landscape was being redrawn to favor new ideological maps very different from the ones he had used to chart his career. He would find a new path and a wider sphere of influence, but of course he didn't know that in advance. All he knew at the time was that he was being hounded out of the very institution he held most dear.

CHAPTER 2

Under the Big Flag

It is impossible to exaggerate how important school was to my father. Like many children of immigrants, he saw education as an essential engine of advancement. Both my parents had used their academic talents to catapult from the economic uncertainty of their immigrant parents, small-time clerks and storekeepers, to the regular salaries and social assurance of white-collar jobs, a transformation they relished but also took for granted. Rising in the world was what happened if you applied yourself at school. But for my father as a child, school was not just a way to get ahead. It was also a source of high ideals and an introduction to a lofty history he hadn't known he shared.

To understand, I turn to a photograph more than a century old. Over thirty-six inches wide and almost twelve inches high, it is too large to fit in any album. Even sideways, it is too long to be legibly reproduced on a standard page. In its entirety, the picture shows the eighth grade graduating class of Bronx P.S. 44 in 1923. Such photographs were common at the time, panoramic portraits of classes, sports teams, and social groups, but this one has fascinated me for many years.

The students stand in the sunlight against the brick wall of their school, ninety-one boys and seventy-two girls in four wide rows, posed in front of a very large American flag that hangs between two windows above and behind them. The graduates are arranged by height, the tallest standing in the rear. In front of the standing students are two broad rows of chairs. Four teachers and the principal sit at the center of the front row, above the identification sign. They are flanked by more students seated symmetrically on either side. The smallest

Grammar school graduation, 1923. The huge flag, only partly visible here, is one of many tools meant to Americanize these children of immigrants. Saul, age twelve, is second from lower right. Credit: Collection of the author.

boys sit cross-legged on the pavement, forming a bottom row in front of the chairs.

On the far-right end of the bottom row, second to the smallest, is my father, Saul. He was never a tall person, but there is another reason why he was shorter than virtually all his schoolmates. The policy of the Board of Education at the time was to "advance" the brightest students, skipping them one or two grades, and "retaining" those who hadn't yet mastered the required curriculum. Saul, only recently turned twelve, would be off to high school in the fall. His classmates in the back row are several years older. A few seem in need of a shave.

Many of the boys in the photo wear belted woolen Norfolk jackets, named after the fifteenth Duke of Norfolk, holder of the oldest dukedom in England, and a favorite garment of those who shoot grouse. Others wear cardigan sweaters, named for the seventh Earl of Cardigan, another member of the British aristocracy who would have been appalled to think of these boys as his peers. Almost all wear pins or badges on their lapels, possibly awards for athletic merit or good attendance. Most of the girls have bobbed hair, and several wear loose white cotton sailor blouses with dark cotton scarves knotted underneath the broad, flat collars. They are not yet flappers, but they will be soon.

Fifteen years before, this Bronx neighborhood had been farmland and the school hadn't existed. By 1923, the newly paved streets are crammed with walk-up apartments for the Catholics from Ireland and Italy and Jews from Eastern Europe who had settled in New York, started families, and sought out less crowded places to live. The two female teachers seated at the center of the photo are pinched and homely, caricature schoolmarms with steel-rimmed glasses and dusty black dresses, collars buttoned to the throat. They appear to be over sixty, which means they were born during or just after the Civil War. The three somewhat younger men seated beside them share the women's look of desiccated toughness, as though all have been slow cured in some educational drying chamber to produce a sort of teacher jerky designed to withstand their rugged journey into the world of twentieth-century urban youth.

The students were proud New Yorkers but also knew their parents were from different countries, and they defended their separate identities with zealous fury. To the teachers, however, they must have seemed very much alike: too loud, too poor, too dark (except maybe for some of the Irish), insufficiently Protestant, regrettably polyglot, and woefully in need of Americanization. People had already begun to describe American society as a "melting pot," and the stated mission of the school system was to turn up the heat, dissolving cultural differences and rendering these children into loyal and productive citizens of the United States. The big flag, only partly visible here, is a tangible part of that program. So are the quasi-military blouses and the pins. Making students memorize the Declaration of Independence helped. So did a graduation pageant my father took part in a few days later, reenacting the founding of New Amsterdam. Naming the school after David Farragut, premier naval hero of the Civil War, was another step in turning these motley urchins into model patriots. The teachers were trying their best, but they do not look happy.

My father, on the other hand, looks ecstatic. There's the excitement of the moment, watching the photographer's panoramic camera rotate on its stand, slowly sweeping across the entire group. There's also the joyful fact that many of the classmates who bullied him daily would be ending their education, starting work and, he hopes, vanishing from his life. For years he has detoured several blocks on his way to and from school, trying to avoid the Irish and Italian gangs that patrol the streets and alleyways, eager to pick fights with the neighborhood's growing population of Jews. Often, he fails. Other kids, including his older brother, fought back, but that was not my father's way. He accepted that getting hit, shoved, chased, and pelted was the price for education. It is worth it, he has already decided. He is good at school. He wants to become a teacher himself.

The boy grinning up at me from his graduation photo learned many things in school, but I'm sure he had no idea of how deeply the hunt for subversives had already affected his education. In 1919, just after the fighting in World War I ended, U.S. politicians became fixated on the recent revolution in Russia, fearful its communist ideology might spread to their own country. Labor strikes across the United States and a series of anarchist bomb plots, some successful and most aimed at government and financial leaders, made the danger of revolution seem even more real.

In 1919, New York State formed a Joint Legislative Committee to Investigate Seditious Activities, known as the Lusk Committee after its red-baiting chairman, Clayton R. Lusk. Labor unions were branded as training grounds for insurrection, and schoolteachers who joined unions were considered active agents of sedition. The Lusk Committee organized raids of the offices of supposedly radical organizations and used earlier statutes against anarchism to expel legally elected Socialist Party members from the state legislature. The Lusk Committee also forced the closure of "leftist" schools (almost entirely in New York City) and sponsored legislation mandating loyalty oaths for teachers and citizenship programs for students. The big flag and historic pageants at my father's grammar school were among the "constructive measures" introduced by the Lusk Committee to battle subversion.

Lusk openly described his committee's work as "repression carried on by and with the consent of the vast majority in the interests of that majority," claiming that "a reasonable and wise repression of revolutionary activities tends toward the maintenance of law, order and peace in the community." New York State governor Al Smith, Irish Catholic and a quintessential child of New York City's melting pot, scoffed at these calls for "reasonable and wise repression." Smith vetoed the new legislation, calling its supporters prejudiced and hysterical and the laws "repugnant to the fundamentals of American democracy."

Smith was defeated in the next election. In November 1919 and January 1920, while the Lusk Committee was promoting repressive new laws, Attorney General A. Mitchell Palmer ordered a national series of raids on schools, organizations, and labor unions with large numbers of Eastern European and Italian immigrants, arresting some three thousand people and deporting over five hundred foreign nationals for allegedly plotting against the United States. J. Edgar Hoover, a rising star in what was then called the Bureau of Investigation, warned of an insurrection planned for May 1, 1920. May Day came and went with embarrassing exercises of police violence and no attempts to overthrow the government, but Hoover's alarms reinforced the existing fear of pro-labor activities.

The New York state legislature successfully enacted the Lusk laws when Nathan Miller became governor in 1921, only to see them repealed when Smith was reelected and returned to Albany in 1923.

What lingered in the minds of many conservatives was the widespread sense that teachers who belonged to unions, or who were immigrants or children of immigrants, were intrinsically suspect and needed to be controlled just as much as their students of similar backgrounds. Remnants of the Lusk laws—flags, pledges, pageants, and other forms of performative patriotism—stayed in the schools, but they were never explained.

I doubt my father knew anything about these conflicts. To him, school was where he could escape family troubles and the warring street gangs of his neighborhood. It was his passport to a safer, better world. In 1923, he believed in the big flag and all it promised. He read library books about military heroes and brilliant inventors, sneaked into silent movies to absorb their dramas of rescue and romance, and assumed that wonderful adventures lay ahead. He had no inkling of what was in store for him or for his country—not the Great Depression of the 1930s, not World War II, certainly not the blacklists, betrayals, and reprisals that shattered the security of his middle years and sent his life in completely new directions. And so he grinned at the camera, his wool knickers pushed above the knee like those of all the other small boys in the front row, ready and eager to fulfill the promise of America.

CHAPTER 3

In the Palace of Education

Public School 44, a four-story brick building with limestone arches over the windows and busts of children flanking the doors, still stands on the corner of Prospect Avenue and 176th Street in the Bronx, still educating the children of the neighborhood. The school opened in the fall of 1910, just six months before my father was born. The man who sits at the center of that graduation photo was Plowdon Stevens Jr., principal from the day the school opened until his death in 1934. The Stevens family history extended back to a Henry Stevens, who appeared on the town rolls of Stonington, Connecticut, in the 1660s, and onward through a long line of soldiers and merchants. Principal Stevens, a champion player of both tennis and chess, was born in Manhattan in 1868, son of a successful owner of warehouses and merchant in lumber and moldings. Unlike many of his peers, he did not go off to Columbia, Harvard, Princeton, or Yale. After graduating from the College of the City of New York (an earlier and smaller version of the institution my father would later attend), Stevens took up a career in the public schools, where he was a strong supporter of military exercises as a way of building student character. I know all this and a great deal more because his father, Plowdon Stevens Sr., proudly compiled a family genealogy that he published in 1909.

My father's family history is not nearly as well documented. Accounts are fragmentary and inconsistent, but it is almost certain that Saul's father, Morris, was born somewhere in the Jewish Pale of Settlement in western Russia around 1880 or 1881 and came to the United States around 1906. Unless, of course, he arrived in 1904 or 1902—the

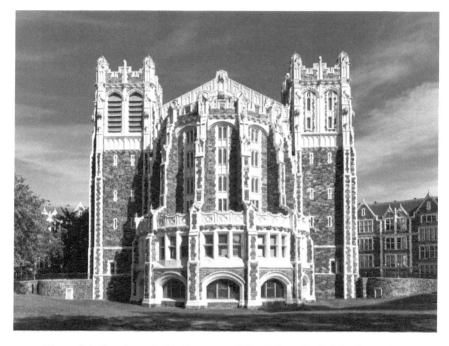

The newly built and proudly Gothic campus of City College. Credit: John Penney / Shutterstock.com.

figure varies from one census to another, and there is no definitive record of his crossing or arrival. Whenever he got there, he was already in New York when he met his future wife. Gittel Wolfe, also known as Gussie, had also been born in Russia, probably in 1886, and arrived in the United States in 1907, the same year they were married. They may have come from the same area, and possibly even the same town, Dvinsk, which would explain why they married so soon after her arrival. In those days, immigrant parents worked as hard to marry off their single children as they had labored to get to America. Legend has it that my great-grandmother, Gittel's mother, seized a broom and chased the doctor from the house after he suggested that a childhood bout of rheumatic fever had so damaged my grandmother's heart that the girl was too weak for marriage and childbearing.

The wedding took place. I have a formal photograph of the young couple and their marriage certificate. Their first child, Leonard, was born in Brooklyn on November 3, 1908, as recorded by the New York City Department of Health. The 1910 federal census locates the family in Philadelphia, where Morris is listed as an unemployed cigar maker. Did they live there or were they just visiting? I don't know. The next official record, the New York State census of 1915, has them living in the Bronx and Morris employed in a cigar store in Manhattan's Murray Hill neighborhood. The building, which still exists, now houses an Indian deli.

Somewhere along the way my father was born, although there is no birth certificate or other record that I or anyone else has been able to find. Over the years, state and federal census takers listed him as Sol, Sam, and even Jane before settling on Saul, the only name he ever acknowledged. Forty years later, Board of Education investigators cited the lack of a birth certificate and the changing records of the boy's name as evidence of the man's unreliable character. Despite the absence of an official record, it is safe to assume my father was a native-born citizen of the United States. My father believed he was born in Brooklyn, like his brother.

Wherever Saul first opened his eyes, he spent most of his childhood in the Bronx, in one of the many walk-up apartment buildings constructed in the first decades of the twentieth century to house the surge of urban pioneers taking the new subways and streetcars out of Manhattan into what had been largely undeveloped land. His parents seem to have missed the classic instruction manual for recent immigrants, with its insistent pressure on the children to succeed, preferably as doctors or lawyers. Gittel grew stout but never very strong, and she let her children grow up as they would. Morris, a man of more style than substance, emulated the elegance of his customers on a cigar store clerk's income. Leonard, the firstborn, found boisterous friends on the streets and grew up to be an amiable ruffian. Saul was consigned to the care of his mother's youngest sister, Frances, only ten when he was born.

Small and round, with chubby cheeks that made him seem even younger than he was, my father quickly decided that school was a haven in a precarious world, and he spent as much time there as possible. Sometimes he arrived so early he was there before the custodians. He would sit on the steps of the Boys Entrance and wait for them to open the doors.

Apart from regular assaults by the more aggressive kids of the neighborhood, Saul had two additional strikes against him that made school both a challenge and a refuge. One started at birth when he was the unwitting contributor to his mother's declining health. The doctor who advised against marriage had been correct in thinking her weak heart would be a problem, as was the doctor who said a second pregnancy would make her a lifelong invalid. My father was not allowed to forget for a moment that it was his fault they always had to live on the ground floor to avoid stairs or, later, that they moved frequently in search of healthier air. The person who most often reminded my father of his guilt was his older brother, Leonard.

Leonard was the second strike. A photograph, taken when Saul was two years old and Leonard four, shows the brothers standing on the stoop of a New York brownstone. Leonard has twisted his cap around to a rakish angle and grins broadly for the camera. My father wears a worried frown, an early indication of his well-justified fear that Leonard was about to hit him, spit on him, or shove him down the stairs.

Leonard cherished his reputation as a street-smart kid, an identity he took with him to school and later into his life as a scrappy but mostly successful businessman. There is an old Jewish custom of giving children a taste of honey on the first day of school, to convince them that learning is sweet. When my father was in grammar school, as they then called the first eight grades, he endured his own somewhat different September ritual. Each year, he claimed, a new teacher would see his last name on the class list, remember Leonard, and give him an immediate hard smack, followed by a warning: "That's for nothing. Don't start." Sometimes they struck him with a ruler, sometimes with an open hand. Probably the words varied, but the message was always the same. They knew he was trouble.

My father would then spend the rest of the fall term convincing the teacher that he was not like his older brother. In the face of this institutional hostility, he became a model student. He absorbed the lessons of the teachers and did his best to mold himself to their expectations, which included learning to write with his right hand.

Whatever the limitations of my father's grammar school, and I'm sure there were many, he was lucky to have started his education in a period of great optimism about the ability of schools to shape working-class children into civic assets. From the late nineteenth century until just after World War I, the fresh winds of the Progressive Era blew through the centers of municipal power in New York City. Educational reformers of the early twentieth century wanted to give public school children the widest possible exposure to what they considered the highest standards of literature, history, science, and the arts, and they wanted it to be free of charge. Academically ambitious children like my father eagerly embraced the curriculum, even if it ignored their own rich cultural heritage in favor of a New England past that had little relevance to their own lives. They felt empowered, as though they were learning a second language that gave them the tools to rise in a meritocracy. It would take a long time to realize the degree to which their membership was always conditional.

Another belief central to the New York City schools of a century ago was that public money spent on education was a good investment, especially for the education of children with few resources at home. Between 1891 and 1924, New York City built over four hundred new public schools, most of them very large. Progressive ideology, swelling populations of immigrants' children, and new state laws that mandated a high school education be available to any student who wanted to continue after eighth grade led to an unprecedented surge of school construction. The new schools were palaces of education, designed to be the physical and ethical bulwarks of a sound society.

The aesthetic grandeur of the New York City schools built from the 1890s through the middle of the 1920s reflects the philosophy of a single presiding architect, Charles B. J. Snyder, who was superintendent of school buildings for the New York City Board of Education for that entire period. Snyder believed that school buildings should have a palatial style that fit their role as both educational and community centers. His buildings had turrets, towers, and crenelated rooflines, entrances that looked like the gates of palaces or manor houses, and interior courtyards like those in which kings and commoners alike had once sheltered from enemy hordes.

Many of these schools have now fallen into decay or been remodeled and subdivided beyond recognition, and it can take a good imagination to recapture the grandeur of Snyder's vision. When they opened their doors, however, the stone carvings over the doors were crisp and clean, the murals on the library walls were bright, and the huge auditoriums, accessible from the street so they could be used for public events, were an awe-inspiring alternative to the cramped apartments of the surrounding neighborhood. Whether the architectural style was Norman French, English Collegiate Gothic, Dutch, Flemish, Beaux Arts, or Jacobean, the idea was the same: this school is a place of honor and prestige.

My father got the message. If he wanted splendor, school was as good as a movie palace and ultimately more rewarding. At a time when many students, including his brother Leonard, dropped out after eighth grade to enter the workforce, Saul proudly entered Morris High School, opened only twenty-five years before and named for Gouverneur Morris, a New York signer of the Declaration of Independence. When the family moved to Brooklyn in search of a healthier setting for his mother, Saul enrolled in what would be the first graduating class at the newly completed James Madison High School, named for the fourth president of the United States. At graduation, he was awarded a gold medal for excellence in English and a scholarship of $100, enough to buy textbooks for the next stage of his education at the towering new campus of the College of the City of New York.

City College, the first tuition-free public college in the United States, had moved twenty years earlier to Convent Avenue in northern Manhattan. This was not just a single castle but an entire fortress of knowledge, a magnificent citadel of academic Gothic architecture designed by George B. Post, architect of the New York Stock Exchange. The new campus commanded the highest point on Manhattan Island, near where Alexander Hamilton had built his country estate, and resembled ancient English universities like Oxford and Cambridge, complete with towers, arches, and gargoyles. In such a place, where first-generation Americans could rise from tenements to become college graduates, it must have been easy to believe that these magnificent buildings promised a respected place in the empire of education.

Saul was sixteen when he enrolled at City College in 1927. Like all his fellow students, he was a commuter, making the eighteen-mile subway journey from the family apartment near Brooklyn's Coney Island. During his freshman year, the school dropped the requirement for classes in military training and added an honors program, two changes very much in tune with my father's interests and ideals.

A career as a high school English teacher seemed both a reasonable goal and a rewarding pursuit for a young man who loved to read. He made new friends, sprouted a blessedly short-lived mustache, acquired a stylish tweed suit, and looked forward to a life spent sharing the redeeming joys of literature with younger versions of himself.

Midway through this fantasy, the world changed. When my father graduated from City College in June 1931, the Great Depression had transformed his prospects. He didn't buy a yearbook, probably because he couldn't afford one, but he did save the program from his graduation. As part of the ceremony, he and his classmates recited the school's Ephebic Oath, modeled on the oath of the Ephebic College in ancient Athens, from which young men had to graduate to attain citizenship. At City College, the graduates recited an oath of devotion to New York City that read in part: "We will revere and obey the city's laws and do our best to incite a like respect and reverence in those about us who are prone to annul them and set them at naught; we will strive unceasingly to quicken the public's sense of civic duty; and thus in all these ways, we will strive to transmit this city not only not less but greater, better and more beautiful than it was transmitted to us."

The pledge to strive for a city "greater, better and more beautiful" than the one they inherited had a special poignance in a time of breadlines and soup kitchens, when homeless encampments dotted Central Park. Saul graduated a year and a half before Franklin Roosevelt's first election as president in 1932 and the ensuing New Deal programs of financial reform and relief. Banks were failing. Unemployment was over 25 percent. Saul's father Morris was driving a milk wagon. His brother Leonard had married his grammar school sweetheart and was struggling to get into the pillow business. His long-suffering mother was in the early stages of the cancer that would kill her three years later, when she was only forty-four. And for the next six years the newly minted college graduate, like much of the nation, could not land a steady job.

The Great Depression didn't destroy my father's desire to be a teacher, but it did make it much harder to reach this modest goal. One of the common stories of twentieth-century Jewish life is that highly qualified people became public school teachers because anti-Semitism closed them out of so many other careers. The story is true as far as it goes, but it assumes there were teaching jobs to be had. There should have been. Across New York City the high schools were packed, creating a teacher shortage, but that meant little if the city just wasn't hiring.

Mayor Jimmy Walker had lined his own pockets but left the New York City coffers close to empty when he abruptly resigned in 1932. Two short-term interim mayors were equally ineffective. Fiorello LaGuardia, who took office in 1934 and served as mayor for the next twelve years, formalized the Board of Education's unofficial system of saving money by not hiring. LaGuardia ordered that the schools hire only substitute teachers—who earned between six and eight dollars a day, had no job security, and were not eligible for sick leave, summer salary, or pensions.

Even those positions were hard to get. My father placed in the top 10 percent of people taking the extremely competitive exam for a teaching license, but in his first six months after graduation, he worked only a total of eighteen days as a substitute teacher across three different public schools in Brooklyn and Manhattan. In January 1932 he began a glorious 153 days of steady employment, stretched over two academic years, at P.S. 51 in the Bronx. Then it was back to next to nothing: one day at P.S. 89 in Manhattan and thirty days at P.S. 80 in Brooklyn. When he was lucky, he taught high school English, his official subject. When he was assigned to an unknown class for just a day or two, he brought a book of adventure stories to read out loud to his restive charges. Between assignments, he picked up jobs as a waiter and busboy.

For almost a year, he found what passed for regular work as a "permanent substitute" at P.S. 35 in Brooklyn. It was a junior high school and he was teaching arts and crafts, but at least it was a job. Twenty years later, when he was under investigation and had no reason to linger after work, he used that early art training to teach me how to draw a face. Start with an oval, he said. Imagine a horizontal line across the middle and put the eyes there (not way on top, as I had wanted). Place the nose at a new mid-line between eyes and chin, and a mouth midway between the nose and chin. To my amazement, it worked. I had drawn a face that looked like a face! If pressed, he would also demonstrate how to create a plausibly proportioned body, using a similar series of ovals and dividing lines. I never saw him draw anything else, but apparently this had been enough to qualify him to teach art.

I know the dismal history of Saul's early teaching career because it was in the records of the Board of Education anti-communist investigation, the file I had received from the Municipal Archives. The only other evidence I have of those years is a small black-and-white photograph, its surface cracked with age. A group of grinning boys in shirt-sleeves perch on a jumble of large rocks, the kind of outcropping that can be found in parks in every borough of New York City. In the center is my father, barely into his twenties. He, too, looks relaxed and happy. His jacket is off, his hair damp and tousled. The hot weather and casual clothes suggest an end-of-year outing. On the back, he had written in pencil, "Jackson Jr. High School. My first Rapid Adv. official class." Rapid Advance was what they called the program through which the brightest students could complete two grades in a single year, usually sixth and seventh grades. Smart kids, eager to learn. Smart alecks, too, no doubt, but that he could handle. Much of my father's later teaching centered on drilling basic literacy into reluctant readers, so a classroom full of able and eager learners must have been a joy.

These long years of substitute teaching were when Saul joined the Teachers Union, a decision that would come to define his career. The Teachers Union was the New York local of the national American Federation of Teachers, established in 1916 to protect elementary and secondary school instructors from arbitrary salary cuts, uncompensated after-school assignments, and unsafe working conditions. One of its founders was John Dewey, the patron saint of progressive education— but also, during his life and long after his death, a villain to the conservative movements that considered "progressive" a synonym for "socialist" and "socialist" a synonym for "communist."

By the 1930s, the Teachers Union was experiencing its own hard times. Leaders were split between those who wanted teachers to focus on social and community issues and those who felt the purpose of the union (apart from the universal issues of hours and wages) was to enhance the status of teachers as highly trained professionals. In 1935, political and professional factionalism split the union. Several leaders who didn't like the trade union solidarity of the Teachers Union left to form the Teachers Guild, taking with them some seven hundred of the approximately seven thousand union members. The remaining officials responded by intensifying their battles to improve low pay and challenging working conditions. Another, more controversial part of the Teachers Union's agenda was the desire to address problems of low-income neighborhoods that were not caused by schools but spilled over into the classroom.

Decent wages, safer working conditions, and an end to systemic racism and economic inequality were also the issues that dominated the public agenda of the Communist Party of the United States of America (CPUSA), which explains a large part of the party's appeal in the 1930s. Many of the leaders of the Teachers Union were indeed members of the CPUSA, which was completely legal and even common at the time. In 1938, for example, the party had 38,000 members in New York State, most of them in New York City, and a CPUSA candidate for president of the city's Board of Aldermen received close to 100,000 votes.

For people like my father, though, joining the Teachers Union had an appeal that came before political affiliations, social action, or conflicting definitions of professionalism. Unlike the Teachers Guild, the Teachers Union offered membership to the swelling ranks of part-time and substitute teachers, pledging to work on their behalf.

CHAPTER 4

A Crash Course in Scandal

At the start of 1937, campaigning for reelection, Mayor LaGuardia lifted his ban on hiring teachers for the city's critically understaffed high schools. Nine newly licensed teachers, including my father, were appointed to the faculty of Samuel Gompers Vocational High School for Boys, a large new school that had opened only two years before. Gompers, who had died in 1924, was being honored as the founding president of the American Federation of Labor (AFL), the first organization to consolidate labor unions representing different skilled crafts in a single, powerful bargaining unit.

Gompers High was another palace of learning, though one streamlined for contemporary machine-age tastes. Its towers were decorated with bas-reliefs of modern-day industrial saints: heroic workers representing trades like wiring, woodwork, drafting, aviation, and the electrical industries. A large mural titled "Power" graced the school library. The boys who attended Gompers High School (and they were all boys) would prepare for a trade, but they would also study more traditional academic subjects. On March 6, 1932, the *New York Times* had published "New Unit to Teach a Whole Industry," describing the proposed new school where students would spend half a day on vocational training and half on "cultural subjects, such as history, hygiene, economics, and so on."

Five years later, the English Department, home to most of the newly hired teachers, was a substantial part of the "so on." In another photograph from the family file, I see my father among his new English

English Department of Samuel Gompers Vocational High School, ca. 1940. Saul sits at lower right. Credit: Collection of the author.

Department colleagues. Still youthfully slender, he has glasses now, with wire rims. His hair is slicked back and his expression is solemn. He wears a double-breasted suit. Finally, after years of waiting, he is a genuine teacher. And he is about to fall into a sea of troubles.

As the new teachers arrived at their new school, they discovered that the timeless realities of greed and fear could overshadow the ideals proclaimed in educational charters and frequently etched into the facades of the buildings where they worked. At Gompers High School it was greed that predominated, at least at first. One of the inspirational credos carved over the school's doors was from Benjamin Franklin, the colonial-era printer who worked his way to wealth and then became a founding father of the new United States. "He who hath a trade hath an estate," the inscription on the entry tower proclaimed. But sometimes, it seemed, plying one's trade was not enough. Fudging the books was another useful way of building an estate.

It didn't take long for the new teachers to notice something very strange at Gompers. Even though New York's schools were still notoriously overcrowded and understaffed, the Gompers principal, Charles J.

Pickett, had hired more teachers than needed for the number of students enrolled. Some newly hired teachers were assigned to sit in empty classrooms. Extra substitute teachers assisted regular teachers, though there seemed to be no need. Along with several other teachers, Saul reported the unnecessary and often idle assistants to the Board of Education, starting almost as soon as he was hired in 1937. And, again, he waited.

During the three years that the official investigation of ghost classrooms inched along, my father found a fuller and more satisfying role for himself at Gompers High. He got a classroom of his own and collected books for a small classroom lending library. When students petitioned for a yearbook, Saul agreed to be the faculty sponsor. Soon he was also supervising the Social Club. He assigned an incorrigible doodler to paint a mural on the classroom wall. He spent his own money on hot rod magazines, passing them out to convince his reluctant students that their dislike of Longfellow and Emerson didn't have to mean the act of reading was necessarily hateful.

Outside of school, life also improved. Saul rented an apartment in a new building with a stylish Art Deco lobby on the Grand Concourse, then an elegant residential boulevard meant to rival Paris's Champs-Élysées. He vacationed at one of the adult summer camps that flourished in the Catskill Mountains and the Hudson River Valley in the years before air conditioning and met a vivacious Hunter College girl, Sylvia Zipser, who was devoting most of her time to the college newspaper. In June 1938, he rode the subway to Brooklyn to get married, carrying his good suit in a bag so it wouldn't get dirty. The newlyweds spent a few weeks in Ithaca, New York, where Saul took a class at Cornell to supplement his teaching credentials and Sylvia fended off the landlady who didn't believe she was old enough to be legally married. Then they returned to the Grand Concourse apartment. Sylvia went back to Hunter for her senior year and Saul to Gompers High School, where more troubles awaited. And he remained an active member of the Teachers Union.

CHAPTER 5

Save Our Schools

What did it mean to belong to the Teachers Union in the years before the United States entered World War II? Much has been written about the political divisions that led to the 1935 creation of the Teachers Guild and to many bitter fights within the Teachers Union over different forms of social activism. Still, the main agenda of the union was simple and timeless: better pay and better working conditions.

Once again, I turn to a photograph, this one hidden for decades in my mystery file. It shows a group of men and women, bundled in winter coats, standing before a building I could not identify. The men wear fedoras or homburg hats. The women have braved the weather in skirts and shoes with sensible heels made for walking, though their hats reflect the whimsical shapes popular in the late 1930s. Many are holding large printed placards of two varieties. One, its text set against a background of the American flag, reads: "The Richest City. The Richest State. Don't Economize on Education." The other: "City and State Cooperate. Save Our Schools." That's the one my father is holding, there on the bottom right of the front row.

Searching for clues about this scene, I went to New York University's Bobst Library, at the southeast corner of Manhattan's Washington Square, to consult Teachers Union photographs now housed in the Robert F. Wagner Labor Archive. I soon realized that the group was demonstrating in front of the New York State Capitol building in Albany, where the state legislature held the purse strings for public schools. I never found a photograph just like mine, but I became familiar with ritual images of demonstrators in front of the State

New York City teachers picket for higher pay outside the state capitol in Albany, ca. 1939. Saul is at lower right. Credit: Collection of the author.

Capitol, its arched windows framing throngs of teachers assembled on its broad steps. Teachers went to Albany many times, always picketing for increased funding. Sometimes they took the train. Sometimes they chartered a bus. On occasion a few top leaders flew on Eastern Airlines from New York Municipal Airport—it was not yet renamed to honor LaGuardia, the mayor who had kept so many of them in the limbo of substitute teaching when he halted all regular appointments during the Depression. Usually they went on days that school was not in session so they could not be accused of leaving their students in the lurch.

Teachers hauled their hopeful placards to Albany in February 1939 and again in 1940, taking advantage of the school holiday that honored Lincoln's birthday, February 12. They were there just before the United States entered World War II, with a banner from the American Federation of Teamsters and signs saying, "Democracy Needs Better

Schools" and "Restore Full State Aid." They returned to Albany five years later under a banner identifying themselves as "Teacher Veterans" who had defended the nation in wartime and signs noting they hadn't received a pay raise since 1928. Other placards demanded a $1,000 annual raise. The next year they were back, now plaintively asking for $900. I never found another photo to match the one in our family file, and I never saw Saul's face in the crowd. But I know he was there at least once, standing with his fellow union members.

CHAPTER 6

Fascist America

While the investigation of the fully staffed but empty classrooms at Gompers High School was slowly moving to its climax, another crisis emerged, one that stemmed from fear and bigotry rather than greed. It started in a small incident in the central schoolyard, a tiny moment that somehow managed to encapsulate the fragile state of American democracy in the months before the United States entered World War II. As would happen so often, my father found himself in the eye of a storm.

Saul's involvement started with two words that I would never have associated with the man I knew: "punch" and "ball." I never saw him hit anyone or anything, including his misbehaving children. I also never saw him do anything requiring physical coordination, let alone play a game in which one was expected to throw, kick, dribble, or catch a ball. The World Series was a nonevent in our house. Football was a dull and violent sport that somehow engaged the attention of many people, none of them worth knowing. Ditto golf. Marbles was the only game I ever heard my father mention that involved a spherical object. And yet it was a student-teacher punchball game that thrust him into the center of a simmering feud at his school.

Punchball, to those who didn't grow up in cities, is an urban cousin of baseball, played with bases, fielders, and "batters," but without pitcher, catcher, or bat. The person who is "up" throws a rubber ball into the air, then punches it into the field and runs to first base. It was a very popular playground game among New York City boys in the first half of the twentieth century (girls played slapball, which is exactly as different as you think).

My father was minding his own business, playing punchball at the end-of-year teacher-student games in June 1939, when the trouble began. Or rather, he wasn't quite minding his business, because the class he was supposedly supervising was playing a different game in another part of the schoolyard. Suddenly, one of his students came running over to report that Timothy F. Murphy, the school's dean of discipline, had shouted an anti-Semitic remark. Angered that boys were sitting on the ground to watch the game, he had yelled, "Get up! Where do you think you are? You're not in synagogue."

In ordinary times, this might have been merely confusing. Many of the students weren't Jewish and sitting on the ground is never part of Jewish observance. But these were not ordinary times, because in June 1939 open anti-Semitism was even more popular than punchball—and much more dangerous.

Although it is not mentioned very often today, a conspicuous segment of the American population was enthralled by Hitler and actively worked to bring his Nazi Party to the United States in the 1930s. In late 1934, Congress learned of a failed plot by pro-fascist, anti–New Deal business leaders to stage a military coup against President Franklin Roosevelt. Starting in 1936, the German American Bund organized marches and rallies across the country, complete with swastika flags, fascist salutes, and shouts of *"Heil Hitler."* Fascist youth groups and paramilitary training camps sprang up across the United States: Camp Hindenburg in Wisconsin, Camp Nordland in New Jersey, and Camp Siegfried, just outside New York City on Long Island, to name just a few. The Silver Shirts, an adult paramilitary group modeled on Hitler's Brownshirts and Mussolini's Blackshirts, held marches and rallies in major cities, with the stated goal of intimidating Jews.

In Los Angeles, wealthy fascist sympathizers went so far as to build a compound in the hills of what is now Pacific Palisades to be Hitler's western headquarters after he conquered North America. In 1939, as tensions rose in Europe, famed aviator Charles Lindbergh advocated a policy of America First, a nonintervention program that was really meant to aid Germany and serve as a thinly veiled platform for anti-Semitism. Lindbergh wanted to limit American cooperation with its traditional allies, England and France, and promote a racist agenda against "non-Aryan" people. He was not alone.

The German American Bund claimed a membership of some ten thousand people. This was much smaller than the estimated 75,000 members of the Communist Party of the United States of America (CPUSA), but many of the CPUSA members were labor unionists, not ideologues, while Bund members were interested in promoting the master race, not improving the wages of working people. And the pro-fascist numbers continued to grow. Conservative business leaders, who condemned New Deal economic regulations as a tool of creeping socialism, supported any attack on unions. Members of the still-powerful Ku Klux Klan saw it as their mission to attack Blacks and Jews individually and as part of any organization to which they might belong, and they often joined with the pro-German forces.

Whether the source was local or national, these attacks often focused on New York City, the port of entry for most Jewish immigrants. In the 1930s, there were over two million Jews in New York State, the country's largest Jewish population, and 90 percent of them lived in New York City. This made the city a tempting site for proto-fascist demonstrations. In February 1939, four months before the Gompers High punchball game and six months before England and France declared war on Germany, twenty thousand people attended a German American Bund rally in New York City's Madison Square Garden to celebrate George Washington's birthday. During the rally, a speaker hailed Washington as "America's First Fascist." James Wechsler, writing in *The Nation*, estimated that the Christian Front, another fascist organization, held at least thirty rallies in New York City in the first half of 1939, many of them with open calls for violence against Jews.

Rallies and parades were one way of supporting fascism. Attacking "the communist menace" was another, and no target was easier than teachers. Father Charles Coughlin, the pro-fascist, anti-Roosevelt, rabidly anti-Semitic Catholic priest based in Royal Oak, Michigan, was one of the most influential spokesmen for the idea that New York City's public education system was staffed by insidious communists.

Coughlin commanded a national audience from his church outside Detroit, using the twin platforms of his enormously popular radio broadcasts (with an audience estimated at thirty million listeners) and his nationally circulated weekly newspaper, *Social Justice*, to lash out at what he claimed was a Jewish conspiracy to undermine the United States. On June 10, 1939, just a few days before Murphy berated Gompers students for acting in ways he somehow associated with Jewish observance, a man was stabbed on the sidewalk in Manhattan by Coughlin's followers when he objected to speakers promoting *Social Justice* with anti-Semitic slogans. Twenty years after Germany's humiliating defeat in World War I, American citizens were actively supporting Hitler's rise to power and embracing the anti-Semitism that was at its core.

Murphy was one of Father Coughlin's many admirers, and his playground outburst was not out of character. He often used anti-Semitic, racist, and anti-Italian slurs against both teachers and students. He was also an active supporter of the German American Bund and the Christian Front. As dean of discipline, Murphy was known for striking students, searching their pockets and lockers, and using verbal abuse to intimidate both students and teachers. His tactics of corporal punishment and public humiliation won him little affection from students. They couldn't wait to report the latest insult when he asked them if they thought they were in a synagogue, making clear he thought a Jewish house of worship was a place of loose, undisciplined behavior.

Teachers had their own reasons to distrust Murphy. He was the person at Gompers in charge of the National Youth Administration, a New Deal agency created to provide paid work experience for students and unemployed young people. Funds were supposed to go to top students, encouraging them to continue their education rather than leaving school for outside work. Murphy was instead using the program to pay his favorite students, not by any measure the top scholars, to cut classes and sell Father Coughlin's anti-Semitic newspaper at the East 143rd Street subway stop. He then demanded that teachers ignore the absences and give these same students high grades.

Murphy had started in the public school system as a shop teacher in 1917 and had then risen into administration. He especially resented the teachers of academic subjects like English and history, sneeringly referring to them as "the college boys." It didn't help that most of the new academic hires were Jewish. Murphy called them "the Jew communists upstairs," since shop classes were usually on the ground floor and the other classrooms above. He was a generation older than the new teachers, and he seemed to feel they needed discipline as much as the students. Murphy seemed very comfortable with the anti-Semitic, anti-progressive bias of the conservative members of the Catholic Church and the militant anti-Semitism of the German American Bund.

My father's problems with Murphy had been simmering since he had arrived at Gompers. As dean of discipline, Murphy was in charge of enforcing standards of good behavior among the hundreds of adolescent boys who filled the classrooms and thronged the halls. Shortly after my father started work, finally elevated to the ranks of permanent teacher, he saw Murphy assault a student, beating him until the boy was brought to tears. When my father tried to file a complaint, the principal turned him away, saying "don't be a fool." Eventually, Murphy's behavior would trigger a city investigation whose records entered the state archives, which is how I know all the details. That was in the future, however. At first, my father's concerns were curtly dismissed. Principal Pickett was a great supporter of Murphy and would soon promote him to the additional positions of chair of the Academic Department, librarian, and acting chairman of the History Department, in spite of his lack of training or credentials for these posts.

Murphy, who also ran the school's free lunch program, denied meals to another student he believed had misbehaved; the student explained to my father that this was why he had nothing to eat. Not long after, another boy came to my father's classroom to clear out his desk, saying Murphy had "kicked him out of school" because he found a pornographic comic book in the boy's locker. Murphy warned my father not to file an official statement of absence.

Vocational high schools like Gompers drew students from all parts of the city and reflected the ethnic and religious diversity of New York, but the students Murphy disciplined all represented groups he didn't like: Italians, Blacks, and Jews. In a crowded study hall in the school library, under the shining WPA mural extolling the miracle of power, he loudly berated an Italian American student before seventy-five of his classmates. When the supervising teacher objected, Murphy announced, "N—— and Guineas come from homes where parents don't give a damn about their kids." On another occasion, he demanded that a teacher replace a Black student that classmates had elected to be student leader, saying "it doesn't look nice" and strongly hinting that the principal agreed with him. When a citywide surge of racist and anti-Semitic incidents in schools led the central administration to urge teachers to include units on tolerance in their lesson plan, Murphy came into a classroom to tell a teacher to stop the lesson. Sounding eerily like contemporary school censors, Murphy claimed that talking about injustice would make students rebellious.

Teachers who objected to Murphy's methods were punished with repeated classroom observations, as many as one hundred for a single teacher in two weeks. Others were stripped of administrative duties and the higher salary that went with them. Meanwhile, Murphy did nothing to stop the posting of stickers within the school urging boycotts of Jewish businesses or the distribution of anti-Semitic leaflets that targeted the Teachers Union.

As far as my father was concerned, then, the playground incident was not an isolated insult. It was the last straw. Saul, twenty-eight years old and full of righteous indignation, again reported Murphy's insult to his principal, the same Pickett who was under investigation for staffing empty classrooms. Pickett was not at all interested in creating another scandal at his school. "Oh, get away, that's all you have to do," Pickett told Saul this time. "Go back to your room. You heard my orders." Instead, the young whistleblower put his grievance in writing, again addressing Pickett. When that got no response, he reported the incident to his union, which was already compiling complaints against Murphy from other teachers and students.

After the Teachers Union entered the fray, the case exploded. The American Jewish Congress, supported by B'nai B'rith, the Jewish fraternal organization dedicated to combating anti-Semitism and other forms of bigotry, began its own investigation of Murphy's ties to anti-Semitic organizations. The Teachers Union presented evidence of Murphy's abusive behavior to the Board of Education in June 1939, to no immediate effect. They then approached Mrs. Joanna Lindlof, the most liberal member of the New York City Board of Education and a strong advocate for unions. Thirteen Gompers teachers signed a formal affidavit testifying to Murphy's abuses.

Soon after the affidavit was submitted, the chair of the English Department, Julius Bernstein, was called to Board of Education headquarters, along with my father, who had not only complained about the playground incident but had earlier tried to bring charges against Murphy for beating students. A third teacher summoned to headquarters was the man Murphy had forced to stop a city-mandated class on tolerance.

Instead of discussing their complaints about Murphy, a panel of assistant superintendents grilled the teachers about their own classroom practices. They were particularly interested, it seemed, in a donated collection of popular novels that had been brought into classrooms for students to borrow—another way of encouraging these budding mechanics and electricians to become more fluent readers. The books had been free, which Bernstein considered an excellent reason for accepting the gift, and he admitted he hadn't read every volume before putting them out. But one book contained an explicit description of a sexual encounter, and the author of another was a known socialist. Instead of being applauded for their efforts to report a physically abusive, anti-Semitic, anti-Italian, racist administrator, the teachers were told that any further unauthorized readings brought into school would get them fired. Meanwhile, the teachers accusing Murphy were being added to the New York State files of possible subversives in the state's employ.

CHAPTER 7

Accusing the Accusers

When school began again in the fall of 1939, Timothy Murphy was still busy doing damage at Gompers High School and New York City was still a center of attacks on Jews in general and Jewish teachers in particular. When France and England declared war on Germany in early September, after Hitler's invasion of Poland, the German American Bund staged another huge parade in Manhattan, complete with rows of goose-stepping marchers holding Nazi flags. In November, Father Coughlin's *Social Justice* featured a lurid headline in the form of a question, "Do Communists Control New York City Schools?" Coughlin's answer, of course, was a resounding Yes!

Social Justice asserted that Mayor Fiorello LaGuardia was a communist sympathizer and that the Teachers Union and its 7,000 members were "the educational wedge of the Communist Party in New York." As proof, Coughlin asserted that the union "is predominantly Jewish, at least 75 per cent of its working committees being of Hebrew extraction." The clear implication was that every Jew was also a communist. Appended to the article was a long list of union officials, with Jew, Jewess, or Gentile after their names.

Coughlin was extreme in his attacks on teachers, but he was not alone. The downstate-upstate divide between New York City and the rest of New York State was also a divide between liberal and conservative, multicultural and homogeneous. The state legislature was dominated by conservative Republicans, and the laws they passed were often aimed directly at curbing the unruly residents of the obstreperous

Father Charles Coughlin's *Social Justice* railed that New York schools were controlled by Jews, who in his view were all communists. Credit: Special Collections, Northwestern University, Evanston, IL. Used by permission of Historical Exploration of Father Charles E. Coughlin's Influence Collection held at the University Archives, University of Detroit Mercy.

metropolis to the south. That was particularly true when it came to laws about education.

In 1939, the same year my father was pushing for an investigation of Murphy, state legislators, building on the legacy of the 1920 Lusk laws, authorized a larger program to police the conduct of liberal teachers. In 1940, the Joint Legislative Committee to Investigate Education in New York State was formed. In the tradition of informally naming committees after their leaders, it was usually known as the Rapp-Coudert Committee, after Assemblyman Herbert Rapp of upstate Genesee County and State Senator Frederic R. Coudert Jr. of New York City, both Republicans.

The mission of Rapp-Coudert was to investigate subversive infiltration of the public schools. Soon after the committee was formed, the New York City Board of Education sent all the material about Murphy to Albany for the committee's use. My father's notarized statement of Murphy's transgressions is in the Rapp-Coudert files, including Pickett's order to "go away," along with many other details of the day-to-day conflicts at Gompers High. The Rapp-Coudert Committee's mandate expired in 1942, but its records were saved. The committee's methods—secret hearings, uncorroborated testimony from paid witnesses, and the assumption of guilt by association—became the model of anti-communist investigations that resumed almost immediately after World War II.

Meanwhile, the protests against Murphy continued. The Rapp-Coudert Committee, like the city Board of Education, was very selective in its investigations, concentrating almost entirely on hunting for communists while ignoring more concrete evidence of fascist influences in the schools. The state committee showed little interest in Nazi sympathizers who were promoting various schemes to sabotage shipyards, organize militias, and pave the way for a German conquest of the United States. The Teachers Union asked why Rapp-Coudert was hunting for communists but not investigating fascists, who seemed to present a more immediate danger to democracy. More specifically, the union demanded to know why neither the state committee nor the city's Board of Education was investigating the fascist at Gompers High.

Larger and larger groups got involved on the side of the Teachers Union, ones less easily dismissed as hotbeds of subversion. The

200,000-member United Parents Association called for Murphy to be censured. In March 1940, Austin Hogan, the president of the powerful Transit Workers Union of Greater New York, with fifty thousand members, wrote to the Board of Education calling for Murphy's immediate removal. "Mr. Murphy, by his racial prejudices, particularly his anti-Semitic, anti-Negro and Anti-Italian expressions and acts, has disqualified himself as a person fit to teach or supervise pupils in a public school system," Hogan declared. Many union members had children in the school system, including at Gompers. Even more union members voted.

The added pressure worked. In April 1940, shortly before the Board of Education finally began hearings about the ghost classrooms, their Department of Investigation also began a formal inquiry on the matter of Timothy F. Murphy, an investigation which lasted over a year.

Among the documents gathered for this investigation was a postcard that seemed to be about recruiting fascist sympathizers. Werner Grunwald was an unemployed radio repairman and member of the German American Bund who had been seen hanging around the German embassy in Manhattan, so it seemed at least suspicious when Murphy wrote Grunwald a postcard saying he would call on him at home in the evening, after which "I will then recommend that you come to school and talk to some of our younger members who are schooled in methods of joining the rank." Was this part of a plan to place Nazi sympathizers in American defense industries when they graduated from high school? Other accusations were that "through his position in Gompers Vocational High School, Murphy has placed some of his trained boys into certain industrial enterprises throughout the country as finger men or skeleton crew for his un-American activities." According to Murphy, his cards to Grunwald were simply attempts to help an unemployed friend get a job on the Gompers faculty.

The transcripts of the official hearings on Murphy would be farcical if the activities they described were not so dangerous. There were debates on whether it was within the rights of a disciplinarian to search student's pockets or keep leaflets he found through those searches, discussions of just how hard an assistant principal should be allowed to hit a student with impunity, and even a long conversation about precisely what part of the schoolyard my father should have been in during the end-of-year games. The teachers who complained about Murphy were labeled as biased, while Principal Pickett declared that Murphy had his full support. What was entirely absent from the debate was any discussion of the larger issue of subversive fascist influences in the school.

While all this was happening, the separate investigation of ghost classrooms slowly moved forward. In June 1940, the Board of Education finally got around to holding hearings about the surplus of teachers at Gompers. Almost immediately, it became clear that the problem was a classic case of financial fraud. Principals of schools with more than fifty teachers were paid $10,000 a year. Principals of smaller schools were paid only $7,500, a full 25 percent less. Having more teachers would also raise the principal's pension, a subject of obvious interest to Pickett since he was nearing the age of compulsory retirement. Gompers had been built to house more students than the initial enrollment. By filling empty classrooms with teachers he didn't yet need, the principal could instantly raise his current and future income. The board decided to suspend Pickett, demote his administrative assistant, and fire the school clerk who had entered data for the nonexistent students.

Then Pickett struck a deal. To spare the Board of Education further embarrassment, he would retire immediately, keeping his inflated pension and the special summer salary owed to him for the months between the start of the investigation in June 1940 and his retirement the following December. As for the teachers who exposed his fraud, many of them were the same teachers who had reported on Murphy's abuses. Instead of applauding them, the Board of Education flagged them as disruptive characters. Not that they knew it.

The Murphy investigation was still going on when Pickett retired. In the fall of 1941, after eighteen months of inquiry, the Board of Education censured Murphy for "reprehensible conduct with respect to teachers and pupils." It declared him unsuited to administrative duties and transferred him to a classroom at another vocational school. To the outrage of his accusers, however, Murphy was soon put in charge of a new program to provide accelerated vocational training for students going into the military. He was even given extra pay because of the newly created assignment.

There is another big surprise in the Rapp-Coudert records of the Murphy investigation. Although the issue at hand was Murphy's objectionable conduct at Gompers High School, the investigation files also contain a handwritten, unsigned list of thirteen teachers alleged to be communists—fully 20 percent of the school faculty. The list includes every teacher who had reported Principal Pickett for financial chicanery or signed the affidavit against Murphy accusing him of violent and often prejudiced treatment of students. It also includes almost every member of the English Department, including Saul Schur.

It did not take much to get on this list. Some teachers were cited as having attended rallies for world peace or fundraisers for veterans of the Spanish Civil War. My father's "crimes" were that in 1939 he was active in the Teachers Union and on the editorial board of the school's union newsletter. The most damning note is that "anon. complainant lists him" as a member of the Communist Party.

How did this list come to be? Apparently, the Board of Education was quite ready to believe that the Gompers High School teachers who were giving the dean of discipline a hard time were part of a larger communist conspiracy to undermine figures of authority, and the Rapp-Coudert Committee was ready to accept that belief. But where did they get their information? It had to come from someone within the school.

One possibility is that Murphy or his supporters anonymously reported his accusers to gain revenge and undermine their charges. Revenge certainly must have occurred to Murphy as he saw what he believed was his good name and long career in the schools smeared in newspapers, union broadsheets, and in the censure that was the investigation's result. Another possible source of this bitter anonymous list was Pickett, the recently departed Gompers principal, who was rumored to have used the two years he was under investigation by the board to compile his own records of the activities, in and out of school, of the teachers who opposed him. The only undisputable fact is that this list of accusations, presented without either attribution or any evidence, made it into the Board of Education records and the files of the Rapp-Coudert Committee, ready to be used again whenever anticommunist crusades resumed.

In spite of the risks, my father continued to burnish what he probably saw as his credentials as an active, honorable citizen. In 1941, just before the United States entered World War II, a popular member of the English Department at City College named Morris Schappes was fired for subversive activities, newly guilty under state laws that also authorized the Rapp-Coudert Committee. Schappes admitted his own membership in the Communist Party of the United States of America—still legal, but now grounds for dismissal from teaching in New York State. Schappes claimed he knew of only four other communists on the faculty—three of whom had died fighting in the Spanish Civil War and another who had left the country. Based on the testimony of informants, Schappes was convicted of lying under oath and was imprisoned for a year.

To my father, a graduate of City College and possibly once a student of Schappes's, this was yet another assault on the freedoms he cherished. Educated to believe in the rights and privileges of democracy and not yet exposed to the full chilling effect of anti-communist committees in Congress, he also believed that outrage was something to be shared. Many others agreed, and there were rallies, student protests, broadsides, and pamphlets supporting Schappes.

In June 1941, the Teachers Union published a thirty-two-page pamphlet called *New York Schools Are Invaded*, with the subtitle "The Coudert Committee: A Spur to Anti-Semitism, a Shield for Pro-Fascists." The pamphlet explained the Schappes case and listed the many offenses of Murphy as an example of the willingness of those in power to allow fascists to "invade" the city schools. Famed anthropologist Franz Boas wrote the introduction and artist Raphael Soyer contributed cover art. William Steig, already a popular cartoonist for the *New Yorker* and later the author of best-selling children's books like *Shrek*, was one of several artists whose drawings lampooned Rapp-Coudert in the pamphlet. There were also letter-writing campaigns supporting Schappes, which gave my father another outlet for his outrage. He wrote to Charles Poletti, then governor of New York, and John J. Bennett, the five-term attorney general, objecting to the treatment of Schappes.

My parents had recently moved to Parkchester, a large new apartment complex in the Bronx, a detailed model of which was featured in the "World of Tomorrow" New York World's Fair in 1939. In this park-within-a-city community, where everyone was a newcomer and eager to meet like-minded neighbors, my father joined the Union Non-Partisan Teachers Club. On behalf of that group, he then wrote to the Parkchester Christian Association, another new organization, suggesting they should join the battle for civil liberties and protest the actions of the Rapp-Coudert Committee.

Instead, the Christian Union passed a resolution supporting Rapp-Coudert—and forwarded my father's letter to the very officials whose behavior he was protesting. Copies of the letters also went to the New York City Police Department Special Service division, charged with covert investigations of possible radicals. At this point, the police entered my father's name on an index card, part of their surveillance of possible subversives that dated back to at least 1919 and that would later be shared with the Board of Education for use in its anti-communist investigations. Like many others, my father did not realize that his protest might deprive him of the very civil liberties he was trying to protect.

A few weeks later, on December 7, 1941, the Japanese attacked Pearl Harbor and the United States entered World War II to fight against Hitler and his allies. The problems at Gompers High School seemed small compared with the global crisis. But that hardly meant the animosities they stirred would be forgotten.

CHAPTER 8

Wars Hot and Cold

World War II rearranged my family in ways that were uncomfortable but could have been much worse. Over thirty years old, extremely nearsighted, unathletic, and by 1942 the father of a baby boy, Stephen, Saul was not anyone's first choice for a combat soldier. For the first two years of the war, he continued teaching at Gompers High, organizing students to collect scrap metal and wastepaper and training them in the reading skills the war effort would soon demand of mechanically minded recruits. When Stephen was born, Saul's students used their time in woodshop to make toys for the new arrival. At home in Parkchester, my father took leadership of a local Boy Scout troop, while my mother abandoned silk stockings and grew bean sprouts in damp trays in the cool dark space under their bed. They were minding the home front.

In late 1943, knowing he would soon be drafted anyway, Saul volunteered for a special program offered to teachers and lawyers from the New York City area. Their mission was to teach basic literacy to Spanish-speaking draftees training as automotive mechanics—an assignment very much like my father's work at Gompers Vocational High School.

The setting, however, could not have been more different. Pine Camp, where my father was stationed, was in northern New York State, eight hours by train from New York City and just a few miles south of the Canadian border. The military base, now known as Fort Drum, was in a region of small farms, deep forests, and heavy snows. Created to train cavalry after the Civil War, Pine Camp was expanded in the

Army instructors outside their classroom at Pine Camp, New York. Saul is seated at lower right. Credit: Collection of the author.

1940s to serve as a training base for the armored divisions under the command of General George S. Patton, with an equal emphasis on tank deployment and automotive repair. Keeping tanks and jeeps rolling was not the base's sole mission. Pine Camp also housed a secret program of acoustic deception producing recordings that, when broadcast, would convince enemy soldiers that tanks or airplanes were approaching. As the project developed, startled residents on both the Canadian and U.S. sides of the border would periodically report sounds of imminent invasion. Another part of the camp held German prisoners of war who were sent out to work at logging camps and local farms—and sometimes asked to sing the old songs for the German grandmother in the kitchen, who would weep with nostalgia and slip the singer a pie. And then there was my father's unit, for which there is very little current information. A photograph shows him standing on the steps of a schoolroom labeled SCSU. The SU stands for Special Unit. The significance of SC is lost.

If it were not for several grainy photographs of military classrooms and the confirming account of a high school friend's father who, coincidentally, had also served there, I might not have believed the Pine Camp Special Unit existed. The stories I heard were of long marches through freezing weather, tales of suffering and military bafflement that seemed to borrow as much from Tolstoy's account of Napoleon in Russia as from personal experience. But it was all true, I was assured by my friend's father. There really was a unit made up entirely of teachers and lawyers from New York City. Yes, their mission was to teach English to Spanish-speaking draftees. No, he didn't recall my father. But two decades after the war, when I heard my father conjure his rusty Spanish to negotiate a car repair in Puerto Rico, I was impressed by his large vocabulary of automotive terms.

Saul's accounts of military service were full of baroque embellishments. His favorite story recounted his efforts to avoid an unwanted promotion. If he did well on the test, he said, he would be transferred to another base and put in charge of other soldiers. If he did poorly, he could spend the final months of his service at Mitchel Field Air Base on Long Island, where soldiers about to be discharged were processed for separation. That was the job he wanted, close to family and far from the grim task of training soldiers for a war that, by then, was already won. But the only way to avoid promotion was to fail the test, and the only way to do that was to know the correct answers, so he could get them wrong.

As my father described it later, you had to prove no aptitude for anything at all to become a baggage handler. Realizing it would take work to make himself into a totally hopeless case, he began to study. In 1935, he had scored near the top of 1,430 applicants taking the exam to be a certified teacher of high school English. Now his goal was to achieve an equally impressive failure.

When, after diligent study, my father scored absolute zero on the exam, he was called in by his commander. To every one of the commander's questions, he answered, "I don't know." The war was ending. The commander had more important business. My father was allowed to become a porter—which was at that moment his highest ambition. For the rest of his service, he was what the army called a discharge specialist, carrying bags for happy survivors at Mitchel Field.

I heard this story many times when I was growing up, but I'm sure it's not entirely true. Saul's military records say he ended the war as an occupational counselor, discussing job options with soldiers about to be discharged. Perhaps he also carried their bags. In any case, his was the version he preferred. It fit his dry sense of humor and his vision of himself as a resourceful survivor. Like wily Ulysses and the heroes of his other favorite stories, he used his wits to escape oppressors. And, as ever, he did it by studying hard.

When the war ended, my father returned to his old job at Gompers High School, where there was a new principal and new dean of discipline. Nazi rallies in New York were a thing of the past. What had survived the war, however, was the old hatred of Jews, immigrants, and organized labor, disparate groups that were frequently lumped together and even more often depicted as dominated by violent political subversives. The schoolyard clashes of the prewar years had become a national crusade against a shadowy enemy shaped more from ideological anxiety than from real existence, at least in the United States. The hunt for subversives, never really abandoned, was about to resume.

Amid deepening distrust of the Soviet Union, an uncongenial ally against Hitler during the war, President Harry S. Truman invited Britain's wartime prime minister, Winston Churchill, to the United

States. On March 6, 1946, in Fulton, Missouri, Churchill delivered his now famous "iron curtain" speech decrying Soviet expansion in Europe. Not long after, Truman addressed the nation with a terrifying vision of the threat of Soviet supremacy, describing communism as an insidious world menace already infiltrating the United States.

There was little reason to trust Joseph Stalin, the murderous leader of the Soviet Union, and undoubtedly there were Soviet spies in the United States, but the crackdowns that followed Churchill's and Truman's speeches do not seem to have been particularly effective—except in creating terror and repression. Truman's most pressing fear, in fact, was losing control of Congress in the upcoming midterm elections and then failing to win reelection as president in 1948. As Roosevelt's vice president, Truman had gained the White House only after the president's death in 1945, and he needed to show that he was as tough on communism as he had been decisive in dropping the world's first atom bombs on Japan.

The result was loyalty oaths, newly empowered congressional investigating committees, and a national surge of anti-communist hysteria. It started with fear of foreign powers and claims of hundreds of Soviet spies within the U.S. government and quickly grew into a broad effort to purge all liberals from television, radio, and film. And then, as had happened before, the investigators came to the schools.

The New York state legislature, led by conservative Republicans, remained eager to join the battle against suspected communist infiltrators. Once again, politicians in Albany focused their attention on teachers. The Rapp-Coudert Committee had been disbanded in 1942, but in 1949 the state legislature passed new legislation known as the Feinberg Law. This law made it possible to dismiss any employee in the state's public school system who belonged to an organization considered by the State Board of Regents to be subversive, with no need to show actual subversive intent on the employee's part. One of these "subversive" organizations was the Teachers Union, of which my father remained a member.

CHAPTER 9

So Many Ways to Offend

As crackdowns on real and alleged communist teachers resumed after World War II, college professors were among the earliest targets. In early October 1948, Norman Mailer, twenty-five years old and suddenly famous as the author of the best-selling war novel *The Naked and the Dead*, took up the issue of academic freedom. He traveled to Evansville, Indiana, to interview the president of Evansville College, a small evangelical institution that had fired a young professor of Bible studies because he had presided at a political rally for Henry A. Wallace, the Progressive Party candidate for president. The rally was not held near the campus and had no relation to the fired teacher's work, but apparently that didn't matter. On October 9 the *New York Post* published Mailer's account of the interview, "Do Professors Have Rights?"

The next day, Mailer joined playwright Arthur Miller, eighty-year-old Black scholar and activist icon W.E.B. Du Bois, Harvard astronomer Harlow Shapley, and other speakers at an Academic Freedom Rally to support educators who "may no longer practice their professions because they dared to exercise their right to speak as citizens," according to the announcement. The rally, held at Manhattan's St. Nicholas Arena on West Sixty-Sixth Street, drew some 2,500 people. My father was among them, and he somehow ended up sitting near the front next to Mailer, two strangers in a sea of rapt listeners. There is no evidence Saul knew he was elbow-to-elbow with a literary celebrity awaiting his turn to speak. Showing up to protest injustice was just something he did.

Over two thousand people gathered at a Rally for Academic Freedom in October 1948 in support of college teachers fired for political activity outside the classroom. Saul, second from bottom right, sits to the left of a very young Norman Mailer. Credit: United Federation of Teachers Photographs, Prior Unions: Box 28, File 519, Tamiment Library and Robert F. Wagner Labor Archives, New York University. Used by permission of United Federation of Teachers.

Rallying for academic freedom wasn't the only way to draw suspicion during the years of anti-communist investigations. In the 1940s and for decades after, supporting racial equality was often taken as a sign of subversive activities. Harry Truman had integrated the armed forces, but Black intellectuals, artists, and political leaders were routinely surveilled by the FBI. In conservative circles, any effort to achieve racial integration or improve conditions for Blacks was considered a communist ploy to undermine the stabilizing pillars of American society. Or, as critics liked to say, "stirring up Negroes to create trouble."

To the prevailing anti-communist thinking, there could be no other reason for white people to care about Blacks, and anyone who thought it had to do with a sense of justice was simply a pawn of sinister forces.

I would like to say my parents were active in the fight for racial equality, but my only evidence is a photograph of my older brother on the front page of a short-lived liberal newspaper, *The Compass*, from August 26, 1949. He was six and we had just moved to another newly completed complex of middle-income apartments, Stuyvesant Town, in Lower Manhattan.

It made sense that my parents saved the newspaper featuring their son on the front page, but I couldn't tell why it made its way into the bewildering accordion file, otherwise exclusively about my father. The first clue was the faces of the other children. One of the best parts of my summer walks with my father was the mix of people we passed. Blacks, Italians, Poles, Chinese, and other excitingly different people crowded the sidewalks of Lower Manhattan. Puerto Rican girls no older than I got to wear earrings and patent leather shoes with—could it be?—high heels. Storekeepers called out to customers in unfamiliar languages. Barbershops had posters in the window featuring styles for hair of a texture that would never grow out of my head. This was very different from Stuyvesant Town, where we lived, and its sister development just to the north, Peter Cooper Village. Of the eleven thousand new apartments, all of them built with the help of public financing, not one was rented to a family of color.

In the *Compass* photo, my brother Stephen is standing at the top level of a metal jungle gym in the small playground just behind our new apartment, gazing into the distance with a nervous look. A Black boy of about the same age peers up from the level below. There is another white boy on the jungle gym, eyes fixed on Stephen, and a white girl who stares straight ahead, clutching a large doll. None of these children seems in any way engaged in play, either alone or together.

The headline, "Everything's Going Along Fine," was wishful thinking. The children on the jungle gym probably had no quarrel with each other, but the real subject of the story was the current attempt to integrate Stuyvesant Town and Peter Cooper Village—a crusade led by a group of activist tenants and vehemently opposed by the building owners, the Metropolitan Life Insurance Company. That summer, a Stuyvesant Town resident had lent his apartment to a Black family, including their young son, Hardine Hendrix Jr., who is shown peering upward in the photograph. The campaign for integration had already led to death threats and lawsuits. Only a few weeks earlier, the New York State Supreme Court had upheld a lower court decision that private landlords could reject tenants based on race. My brother would stay, but the Black boy perched below him on the jungle gym would soon be forced to move away.

The defendant in the court case was not some small landlord suing for the privilege of choosing who would share his living space. The Metropolitan Life Insurance Company, now known as MetLife, also owned Parkchester and other planned communities in New York, Virginia, and California. During the war, my mother and older brother had left Parkchester for a one-bedroom apartment in Manhattan, where my father joined them when he was discharged from the army. When they had the chance to move to Stuyvesant Town in 1948, shortly after I was born, they happily expanded into a sunny three-bedroom apartment on the southern edge of the new complex.

Stretching from 14th Street north to 23rd Street and from First Avenue east to Avenue C, almost to the East River, Stuyvesant Town and Peter Cooper Village contains 110 redbrick apartment buildings thirteen to fifteen stories tall, transforming a previously shabby part of Lower Manhattan. Named for Peter Stuyvesant, the last Dutch director-general of what was then New Amsterdam, and for Peter Cooper, the nineteenth-century inventor and industrialist who founded the tuition-free Cooper Union a mile to the south, the adjacent complexes boasted parks and playgrounds, decorative fountains and plazas, and curving interior streets lined with saplings that would soon grow into trees.

MetLife had been granted eighty acres of prime Manhattan real estate for its new apartment complex. The land deal was based in part on the promise of easing the city's postwar housing shortage, with special preference for housing military veterans. As far as management was concerned, however, the pledge to house veterans stopped at the color line. There was also said to be an unofficial policy of grouping tenants by religion, with different buildings housing predominantly Protestant, Catholic, or Jewish residents, but that could not be proved. On integration, however, MetLife was open in its opposition. As the company president, Frederick H. Ecker, told the *New York Post*, "Negroes and Whites don't mix."

New York City's Black population had increased fourfold since 1910, and housing shortages were even more extreme in Harlem and other primarily Black enclaves than in the rest of the overcrowded city. A survey of 25,000 residents of Stuyvesant Town and Peter Cooper Village showed that two-thirds opposed the whites-only policy. But when a group of tenants took the landlord to court, MetLife won.

As far as I know, my parents were not among the volunteers who protected the Black tenants or agitated on their behalf. My father and mother believed in the principle of racial equality but had no close friends or colleagues who were Black. Beyond the chance encounters of city life and the important exception of Pearl Keys, the Black housekeeper who entered our lives a few months before I was born and now commuted each day from West 113th Street to keep my parents dual-career household from falling into total chaos, I had had little real contact with the Black or Brown inhabitants or New York. And yet Saul and Sylvia proudly saved this proof of their son demonstrating how easy integration would be.

Decades later, reading the cherished copy of *The Compass*, I was reminded again of how everything in that postwar decade seemed to come back to the pervasive fear of communism. The staged enactment of an integrated playground was on the front page of *The Compass*, but only "below the fold," a secondary feature on the lower half of the page. The top story that day concerned events at the federal courthouse in Lower Manhattan's Foley Square, two miles away. Eleven national leaders of the Communist Party of the United States were charged with advocating the overthrow of the American government, an accusation they vigorously disputed. The trial, overseen by Judge Harold R. Medina, had already lasted over six months. It would set the tone and terms of the anti-communist hearings of the next decade, with assumptions of guilt by association, assertions that an opinion could be a crime even if never followed by a criminal deed, and the generous application of contempt citations to both defense lawyers and plaintiffs.

The surprise witness at the Foley Square trial was a Massachusetts advertising executive and Baptist youth minister named Herbert Philbrick. Philbrick's public life was coupled with his secret membership in the Communist Party and his even more secret work as a double agent for the FBI. In 1940, Philbrick had joined a communist-affiliated youth group in Cambridge, Massachusetts, decided he didn't like it, and called the Boston office of the FBI to volunteer his services for what became years of undercover work. His 1949 testimony at the Foley Square trials led to convictions for the eleven people accused of subversive activities. Having gone public with his undercover work, Philbrick was also free to write his successful 1952 book, *I Led 3 Lives*, which was followed a year later by an even more popular television series of the same name.

I go back to the playground photo. Was it, too, a sign of communist infiltration? The third boy perched on the climber lived in our building and was the older brother of a girl who would be my earliest childhood friend. His father, another City College graduate, would also be blacklisted a few years later and would lose his job teaching at Brooklyn Technical High School. Does this mean that he, his wife, my parents, and the parents of the other children in the photo were communists together, exploiting their children to undermine the freedom of Metropolitan Life Insurance to impose racial segregation on housing financed in part by taxpayer funds? Had the photographer, who may have worked with my mother early in her career, called in a favor and asked her to round up some kids for his picture? Or were the children simply hanging around the playground outside our apartment, captured by a journalist in the days before consent forms? Like so much else, the answer to this question is lost beyond retrieval. But those same children and thousands of their young neighbors soon became the cause of another crisis.

CHAPTER 10

A Seat for Every Child

By the time the Board of Education began its most methodical pursuit of alleged subversives in the 1950s, Saul was not just a teacher, an army veteran, and a member of the Teachers Union. He was also the father of two children, one already in school and one soon to enter kindergarten, and he was bitterly dissatisfied with local school conditions. Furthermore, he was determined to act. Finding out about his clashes with the Board of Education in his role as a parent was just as surprising to me as discovering he had been investigated as a possible subversive.

New schools. More classrooms. More teachers. Fewer building hazards like peeling lead paint or crumbling bricks. All of these were part of the Teachers Union agenda, which immediately made such demands suspicious to school officials hyperalert to any signs of a left-leaning ideology. To the parents of Stuyvesant Town and Peter Cooper Village, good schools and adequate classroom space were nonpartisan issues, fundamental to the pursuit of happiness that so many of them had risked their lives to defend in the global war that had ended only a few years before. As returning soldiers embraced the peacetime mission of making families, the priority for veterans in getting apartments in Stuyvesant Town and Peter Cooper Village turned eighty acres of Lower Manhattan into a vast baby nursery, part of the population explosion soon referred to as the Baby Boom. The problem of inadequate classroom space hit when all those children got old enough to go to school.

PTA leaders from three different schools campaign for new schools as Stuyvesant
Town and Peter Cooper Village overflow with Baby Boom children. Saul is at lower
left. Credit: Collection of the author.

After the great burst of school construction during the first decades
of the twentieth century, both new buildings and routine maintenance
had lagged during the economic depression of the 1930s and the ration-
ing of metal and other construction material during World War II.
When massive numbers of new babies started arriving, it was easy to
predict that they would be starting school in a few short years. Pre-
dictions, however, do not create classroom seats. In 1950, an investigation by the *New York Times* showed that New York City would have to
open fifty new schools a year over the next five years to house
expected enrollments, but city budgets planned for only half that number. No money at all was allotted to fix a sixty-million-dollar backlog
in repairs for all the unsafe and antiquated schools that would remain
in use even after new construction.

School overcrowding was especially acute in our neighborhood in Lower Manhattan. Stuyvesant Town and Peter Cooper Village had been designed for families. Unlike the walk-up tenements they replaced, including some without indoor plumbing, the new buildings had elevators—bright enamel boxes colored red, blue, or green like a starter box of crayons. They had laundry rooms with washers and dryers and special basement storage areas for baby carriages. Many of the apartments had three or even four bedrooms, and separate playgrounds, some for toddlers and some for older children, were easily reached from every building. *Town & Village*, an independently owned newspaper that detailed every aspect of life in the new apartment complexes, regularly printed a community calendar brimming with activities for children. There were preschool programs every day at one or another of the twelve playgrounds, and supervised soccer, touch football, basketball, and arts and crafts for older children. Photographs of adorable toddlers appeared frequently among the ads for furniture stores, diaper services, clothing stores, and other local businesses.

Somehow, though, while building their bucolic town and village, neither MetLife nor the city had done anything to provide schools for the 100,000 new families who would soon arrive in the neighborhood. In fact, they had razed two of the existing neighborhood schools. One of the remaining two elementary schools was P.S. 19, on Second Avenue and Fifteenth Street, built before the Civil War and frequently cited for health violations, including its single basement toilet. The other elementary school was P.S. 61, on Twelfth Street and Avenue B, a five-story brick behemoth that opened in 1913 with a capacity of 1,400 children. Over the next forty years, the immigrant population of the Lower East Side shrank to less than half of what it had been when the school was new, and the building received little maintenance as it served the remaining families of the Lower East Side. Then came Stuyvesant Town and Peter Cooper Village, along with the nearby Jacob Riis Houses, a 1,200-apartment public housing project, all of them bursting with kids.

P.S. 61 was the school my father and I passed so often in our walks. Although I didn't know it until I started exploring the puzzling contents of my newly discovered family file, he was president of its PTA and deeply engaged in the fight to relieve overcrowding. Instead of keeping a low profile when the New York City Board of Education was cracking down on liberal-leaning teachers, Saul was leading a group of organized and impassioned parents lobbying that same Board of Education for new schools.

The P.S. 61 PTA was not a demure group that held bake sales to raise money for sports teams or art supplies. It was an activist organization that sponsored lectures on child psychology and family planning, collaborated with the local health department to promote vaccinations and free X-ray screenings for tuberculosis, and publicly fought the Board of Education for bigger, newer buildings that would, at a bare minimum, meet the legal requirements for health, safety, and hours of instruction.

Another school my father and I often passed was Immaculate Conception, a block away from our apartment on the other side of Fourteenth Street. I marveled at the girls in their plaid uniforms jumping double Dutch in the playground, two ropes swirling in opposite directions in an intricate game I thought you had to be Catholic to master. I should have marveled at the playground itself. As I would soon discover, there was nothing like it at P.S. 61. But we were not Catholic and my parents, like the majority of parents in our community, wanted to send their children to public school.

Learning that my father led the battle to expand neighborhood public schools was another lesson that made me revise my image of the man I knew as a detached observer of the world's follies. Saul took over the job of PTA president a year before he was pushed out of his job, but he already had many reasons to question the simple stories of democracy and patriotic duty that had been such a big part of his lessons as a child. Still, he never doubted the central importance of the public school as both a center of learning and a center of community action.

I never heard a word of criticism of the school I was about to enter, crowded though it was. Only much later did I realize how bitter the fight had been, how centrally my father was involved, and how much both of us were being schooled in the fraught realities of education. His years as a teacher provided many lessons in disillusionment, but he wanted my years as a student to be as full of wonder as his own had been. At the very least, he wanted me—and thousands of other children—to have a chair to sit on.

To find out more about my father's role in the fight for new schools, I had to read the coverage in *Town & Village*. Although this weekly newspaper has considerable historical interest, only a few scattered issues have made it into library collections. To read more, I took the commuter train from Grand Central Station to New Rochelle, New York. Hagedorn Communications, publisher of *Town & Village*, *Co-Op City News*, *Real Estate Weekly*, and other hyperlocal newspapers, used to be in Lower Manhattan but had long since moved over the border to Westchester County. The company now occupies the former site of the New Rochelle Public Library, a building I had visited many times after my family moved from Stuyvesant Town to New Rochelle when I was in fourth grade. The worn marble stairs that had led upstairs to the forbidden realm of adult fiction now took me to a crowded office that held the only existing archive of *Town & Village*. Poring over the bound volumes of crumbling newsprint, I saw my father's name in nearly every issue of 1952 and 1953. The subject was always the need for more classrooms and new schools.

The fight for more classrooms began almost as soon as the new housing complexes opened. In 1950, parents in the district conducted a door-to-door survey of how many children would enter school in the next two years, but the warning of imminent overcrowding spurred nothing more than vague promises of future action. Projected enrollment for 1952–1953, the year I was to enter kindergarten, was 2,000, almost 50 percent over capacity. According to at least one report cited in *Town & Village*, my class and the grade above me would have the largest kindergarten and first grade enrollment of any single school in the world.

Money for new schools flickered in and out of proposed city budgets, never staying long enough to lead to any actual construction. In January 1952, the Board of Education assured my father in his role as president of the PTA that the site for a new school had been approved for purchase, but in February the approval had been sent back "for restudy" to George Pigott, assistant superintendent for housing, the man in charge of all the school system's buildings. Pigott had been one of the assistant superintendents who grilled my father and two other teachers before the war, and he would come back to haunt him.

A delegation of P.S. 61 parents met with Pigott in February 1952 and came back complaining they were getting "a run-around." By May, the runaround had turned into a flat rejection. It was more important to build a new junior high school, the elementary school parents were told. Both were needed, the parents insisted, and another new elementary school as well. And meanwhile, no schools at all were being built in the area.

To my father, the fight for new schools brought back the painful lessons of the prewar scandals at Gompers High School, and especially the realization that private assurances meant nothing and delays were a weapon for those in power. In this new crisis, public outcry and swift responses were needed. By the spring of 1952, our Stuyvesant Town apartment became an ad hoc publishing office where my father churned out newsletters, instructions to parents, and letters to school and city officials. The mimeograph machine was somewhere else, but the big desk in my parents' bedroom was strewn with flimsy blue stencils, typed up and ready for the duplication and distribution. Parent volunteers again went door to door, this time handing out preprinted postcards, recruiting their neighbors to sign and mail the card urging elected officials to ease the crisis of overcrowding. My father was also typing formal letters on PTA stationery, mailed to the Board of Education and shared with our weekly newspaper. *Town & Village* knew enough about their subscribers' interests to provide a blow-by-blow chronicle of our very local school construction war.

In May 1952, writing to the city as president of the PTA, my father cited the severe overcrowding, the projection for even more students in the year to come, and the difficulties of double and triple sessions, particularly for the lower-income parents of the Jacob Riis Houses. Over a thousand parents of the Jacob Riis Houses sent a petition to the New York City mayor demanding a new school; the petition was "promulgated by the Riis Mothers Club in cooperation with the P.S. 61 PTA," according to *Town & Village*.

The battle continued after school let out for the summer. In June, parents from four different schools packed the P.S. 61 auditorium to share information and coordinate efforts for increased classroom space, resolving that they should not fall into the trap of competing against each other for needed construction. Fed up with the lack of progress, the united parents formed committees to visit the city planning commission, local officials, and political leaders. The parents of Stuyvesant Town and Peter Cooper Village, most of them military veterans and their families, were up in arms.

Headlines in national newspapers that summer featured the Rosenbergs' appeal, the successful Republican effort to draft Dwight D. Eisenhower for president, and the death in Argentina of Eva Peron. In *Town & Village*, the headlines were almost always about the battle for more classrooms. A parent delegation to a July 2 meeting of the Board of Education arrived with graphs, mounted on poster board, citing the board's own figures about overcrowding. On July 17, more parents attended the city's Board of Estimate meeting, where they learned that at least there would be money to buy furniture for P.S. 40, serving the north side of Peter Cooper Village, where elementary students had been sitting on folded newspapers on the floor because they didn't have desks or chairs. The combined PTAs again presented detailed summaries of the Board of Education's own surveys of present and future school attendance, noting over three hundred students who had mysteriously vanished between reports. A Board of Education spokesman, defending the undercount, was quoted in *Town & Village* on August 21 as saying, "You would have to have a Ouija board and crystal [ball]" to know how much enrollment would surge from the year before. Hardly. A moment's glance at city population figures would have been sufficient.

Still, the delays continued. Chairs were possible, sufficient space to use them was not. Funds for an additional new elementary school were included in the city budget. Or might be included. Or should be included. Sites were considered, approved, reconsidered, then rejected. Construction was an urgent priority, then a secondary goal, then eliminated from consideration. As I read these accounts of constant activity, I began to suspect that my summer walks with my father had also included prospecting for possible building sites.

The summer of 1952 turned into fall, and school began with no relief for classroom overcrowding. I said I was looking forward to starting kindergarten the year my father was being investigated by the Board of Education. That doesn't mean I knew for sure that I could go, because I was below the age of required school attendance. Throughout the summer, I pestered my parents to know what would happen to me in the fall, only to be told we would have to wait to find out. When we finally got the news that I could enter kindergarten, just a week before school started, my parents were so grateful they saved the letter, another relic I discovered in my mother's files.

Now that I've seen this letter, outlining with exquisite precision the many tiers of admission, I know my chances for starting kindergarten had not been good. I was several months shy of my fifth birthday, in the very lowest group of eligible children at a school that was already filled far beyond capacity. Maybe it was a special favor because my father was president of the PTA. Maybe the principal, Max Francke, had decided that there was no point in trying to limit enrollment in his already wildly overcrowded school. Whatever the reason, I started kindergarten in September, along with far too many classmates.

Because there were so many more children than space allowed, classes ran on an intricate schedule of split grades and staggered sessions, all duly recorded in *Town & Village*. Students arrived and departed at different times throughout the day, each change accompanied by ringing bells and milling crowds in the halls. For kindergarten through third grade, classes began at 7:55, 8:20, 11:20, 11:30, 11:50, or 12:30, and ended at 11:30, 12:00, 12:30, 2:30, or 3:30. Lunch, recess, assemblies, and other nonacademic activities had all been eliminated. Hallways were patrolled by children in the upper grades, charged with hurrying the little kids out of classrooms and then hurrying the next group in. No child received the full number of instructional hours required by law. Parents were distraught, especially the ones who had several children on entirely different schedules. And they were more than ready to keep up the pressure on officials.

CHAPTER 11

Life Comes to School

Six weeks after I started kindergarten, the October 8, 1952, issue of *Life*, the glossy news and photo magazine with an enormous national readership, devoted four pages to a story titled "A Principal's Ordeal." In words and pictures, it traced the harried day of Max Francke, the P.S. 61 principal. Twenty-three photos, timed from 7:50 in the morning to well after the last dismissal at 3:30 in the afternoon, showed Francke moving through packed classes and crowded hallways, dealing with lost children, exhausted teachers, frazzled mothers, and the intricate choreography needed to keep all those bodies moving in and out of their shared space. The editors of *Life* declared P.S. 61 "the most over-populated school in New York," and warned that managing such a schedule is "likely to bring him ulcers or angina pectoris. Three of his friends and fellow school officials have already dropped dead of heart attacks this year."

Leonard Sussman, a photographer for *Life*, was also a P.S. 61 parent and may have been the force behind the coverage, but the story played out on newsstands and magazine racks across the nation and was delivered to the homes of thousands of subscribers. Although neither my father nor the PTA he led were mentioned in the *Life* feature, they made sure the Board of Education and the Board of Estimate were aware of how true the story was.

Maybe some of the children who swarmed the six morning and six afternoon sessions of kindergarten, forty or fifty to a class, realized the shortcomings of their crowded days. I certainly did not. Having no idea what a "normal" school day was supposed to be, I accepted the situation without question. The only thing I was sure of was that school—both the concept and the fact—was enormously important. It would take decades for me to learn about my father's battles and realize that some of the troubles they caused were, in fact, for the sake of my education, in which he believed so fervently.

Compared to the nursery school I had attended, kindergarten was an endless source of fascinating novelties. Instead of walking through the interior byways of Stuyvesant Town to the basement of a brownstone house on Third Avenue, I now got to cross the perilous and thrilling thoroughfare of Fourteenth Street and walk past the enticing storefronts of Avenue B, where boxes of tropical fruits, housewares, pink Spalding Hi-Bounce rubber balls, and tiny packets of bubble gum all shared the display space near the front. I was now able to line up with the big kids to enter the crowded fortress that was P.S. 61, with its exciting scars of wear. On hot September days, our teacher would summon a tall boy from one of the older grades to use a long pole with a hook on the end to open the windows and allow in some air. When the breeze blew, we could sometimes smell the lingering aroma of the abandoned stables across the street, horseless now but still fragrant. Other times we smelled each other, forty little children packed into a single class, our jackets crammed into an ancient cloakroom suffused with the dusty, slightly sour air of decades of winter woolens. Of the following grades, I remember almost nothing, but kindergarten made a vivid impression.

I doubt I learned much in such a short and chaotic day, at least by normal academic measures. Some of my classmates spoke Spanish, Polish, or Chinese instead of English, but we could all sing songs, practice counting, and memorize a strange incantation called the Pledge of Allegiance, addressed to the flag hanging on a wooden pole in the corner. Like almost all children, I garbled the words, most of which I didn't understand. I had no idea what "allegiance" meant, or "pledge." When we got to the part about "the republic for which it stands," I thought of the farm stands my mother liked to visit on country drives and concluded these were stands that sold something called whichits. But I knew we had to learn the words and stand to recite them every morning at the start of class, right hands pressed over our hearts.

That was probably the most important lesson of the year: acting in unison, modeling patriotism before we even knew the meaning of the words. The Pledge of Allegiance had been written in 1892 by Francis Bellamy, a Baptist minister who believed in socialism, but it had long since been seized by conservatives as a litmus test of "proper" thinking. Both in setting and in content, my class was very similar to my father's experience thirty-five years earlier—but shorter and more crowded. Like him, I was being schooled in national loyalty, protected from a danger I neither knew nor sensed.

A second lesson, closely aligned to the morning ceremony of saluting the flag, was that the beloved country to which we pledged allegiance (whatever that might mean) was in great danger. Fear of communists in the classroom, so central to my father's problems, was intensified by fear of nuclear war after September 1949, when the Soviet Union tested its first nuclear bomb. Kindergarten was when I learned to crouch in the hallway, facing the wall with my head between my knees, as the wail of sirens pierced the air. These air raid drills were an ordinary part of school, far more frequent than games or field trips— so ordinary, in fact, that I was surprised to learn they had been dropped by the time my own children entered school.

Air raid drills were only one way to prepare schoolchildren for nuclear attack. In 1951, while parents across the city were clamoring for more desks, more chairs, more classrooms, and more schools, the New York City Board of Education spent $87,000 on identification necklaces that looked exactly like the dog tags worn by soldiers in World War II. By February 1952, the city had invested another $70,000, purchasing a half million ID tags that were given free of charge to children in every school. The tags were a silent admission that ducking under furniture or covering our heads with our hands would not offer much protection from nuclear attack. Like our fathers, so recently back from military service, we schoolchildren needed tags to identify our corpses. My brother Stephen had a dog tag, of which I was very jealous. I had hoped to receive my own when I entered kindergarten, but apparently the program had been abandoned by then.

For many parents, crowded classrooms and fractured schedules were a more immediate threat than nuclear bombs, and one they could try to avert through personal action. During my first year at "the most overpopulated school" in the city, my father continued to rally his parent troops. They harangued Manhattan Borough President Robert F. Wagner, who would be elected mayor the following year. They sent letters and telegrams to the chairman of the city planning commission. In September, shortly after school began, they brought Wagner, along with newspaper reporters, photographers, and representatives from the Chamber of Commerce, to tour their crowded and decrepit schools.

That tour of horrors, reported in the September 18 issue of *Town & Village*, combined with the embarrassing national exposure of overcrowding featured in *Life* magazine a few weeks later, seemed to have an impact. Construction of a new elementary school was moved from lowest priority to second highest in the city's proposed construction plan. But parents knew that proposals meant nothing if money for the new school was not in the city's budget. It was time for a show of force.

The city planning commission was holding an open hearing on the next year's capital budget on October 17, 1952. Over 1,000 parents from Stuyvesant Town and Peter Cooper Village boarded chartered buses, taxis, and the subway to reach City Hall, jamming into the Planning Commission hearing room and overflowing into the halls. They were there to demand that the new junior high school and two new elementary schools they had been promised would in fact be funded and built. A month later, thousands of parents returned to City Hall for the open budget hearing of the Board of Estimate.

The front-page photo in *Town & Village* on October 23, under the headline "Angry Mothers Demand New Schools," shows a sea of women, some with children in hand. At their head is a single man. Robert Konove, a Stuyvesant Town resident with a private law practice and two children at P.S. 61, was chair of the PTA's Legislative and School Construction Committee—not a post included in most PTA rosters. His daughter Jill was my kindergarten classmate. In the corner of the picture, his back turned, you can get a glimpse of my father—clearly visible to the mothers but almost hidden from the photographer.

Konove was an eloquent spokesman. He brought graphs and charts and was not shy about correcting city enrollment figures. He didn't hesitate to describe the Board of Education's dismissal of the need for new schools as a distortion of fact which, "if not willful," was the result "of gross incompetence or stupidity." Konove had another quality that made him a good spokesman for these confrontations: he was not an employee of the Board of Education and therefore safe from reprisals.

The fight for new schools continued through the heated national and statewide political campaigns of 1952, which ended in an election that gave the Republican Party control of the presidency and both houses of Congress for the first time in twenty years. Eisenhower campaigned for president on the memorable, meaningless, and very effective slogan "I Like Ike." The Democratic candidate was Illinois governor Adlai Stevenson, a liberal and internationalist who was known for his wit and keen intelligence, qualities turned against him when Republicans stuck him with the disparaging descriptor "egghead." Most of the adult men living in Stuyvesant Town and Peter Cooper Village had served in the military when Eisenhower was supreme commander, and the Republican Party was active in the neighborhood. Undaunted, the Stevenson campaign sent a motorcade of twenty cars to bring residents to hear Stevenson speak at Madison Square Garden.

It is the first political campaign that I remember. Winter, with its hated woolen leggings, had not yet arrived, but the weather was cool enough for my brother Stephen to say we should stand where the angle of our building made a sheltered corner, out of the wind blowing off the East River and down Fourteenth Street. We were waiting for our father to pull our dark green Studebaker sedan around from the side street where he had parked. The presidential election would be in a few days. I sang a ditty I had heard other children sing at school that ended with the shout, "I like Ike!"

"No, you don't," my brother said, with all the condescending boredom of his ten years. Since his birthday, he had been six years older than me, but soon I would turn five and he would still be ten. After the election.

"Yes, I do," I insisted. "Mommy and Daddy do, too. Everybody likes Ike! I know it!"

"No, they don't," Stephen said in the same dismissive tone as before. "You don't know anything."

All older brothers dismiss the wisdom of little sisters, but I was particularly crushed to think that I might be wrong about one of the first things I had learned at school, even before I had quite mastered the Pledge of Allegiance. Young as I was, I knew that school was very important to my parents, and it was deeply troubling to think I had misunderstood this early lesson.

CHAPTER 12

Man of the Year

Stevenson was not elected president, but my father was happier with the results of a different election a few weeks later. I was halfway through kindergarten when *Town & Village* announced the results of its annual "Man of the Year" competition to honor the civic achievement of a resident of Stuyvesant Town and Peter Cooper Village. For the first time, the honor went not to an individual but to a group: the 1,760 parents whose organized and persistent action over the past three years had finally resulted in funding for new schools. It had been a long struggle, but finally the pressure—the surveys, charts, postcards and pamphlets, outreach to glossy magazines, mass attendance at city meetings, and shaming tours of decrepit buildings—had worked. An additional elementary school was promised to the P.S. 61 district, a new junior high school in the P.S. 40 district, and improvements to the existing P.S. 19, an 1859 elementary school that had multiple health and safety violations but continued to be used.

Even as they celebrated, Saul rallied the parents for one more battle. Just before the award ceremony, he had learned that the site promised for their new elementary school was instead being sold to the Yellow Cab Company to use as a taxi depot. Abraham Beame, the city budget director (and future mayor), was determined to go through with the sale, once again postponing construction of the new school. Beame controlled the city purse strings and was accustomed to canceling projects he considered too expensive, even in the face of well-established need. What was more disturbing was that George Pigott, the Board of Education's assistant superintendent for housing, the man in charge of school construction, seemed to agree. Pigott, who had given parents "the run-around" two years before, was now completely reneging on official promises. The reasons were unclear, but to my father, now so finely attuned to financial chicanery, the reversal seemed very suspicious.

As he accepted the Man of the Year award on behalf of P.S. 61, my father urged the audience not to give up in the face of this new set-back. In a speech that earned a separate column in *Town & Village*, he urged the assembled parents to rally once again. They must come in the hundreds to upcoming meetings of the Board of Estimate and the Board of Education. They must again write to their elected representatives and make their voices heard.

Saul's work as a public school teacher and as a campaigner for better public schools were two facets of the same devotion to education—or, as some saw it, two identifying signs of a troublemaker who must surely have subversive ties. Even as my father was leading his fellow parents in the crusade for new schools, he was being squeezed out of the classroom. Since September, he had languished in a professional purgatory, not quite fired but relegated to a job that left him essentially idle. Without explanation, he had been transferred from Gompers High School to the High School of Aviation Trades, a different vocational school then located in Manhattan.

It's not clear what, if anything, he did in the classroom during the 1952–1953 academic year. At Gompers, he had been an active member of the English Department and a willing advisor for after-school activities. When Gompers enrollment outgrew the main building, he agreed to sponsor a new publication, the *Gompers Echo*, produced entirely by students in the new Gompers Annex. Annexes, classes held in vacant buildings often several blocks away from school, were the Board of Education's favorite solution to overcrowding. When the first issue of the *Gompers Echo* came out, the assistant principal wrote Saul a memo of congratulations, noting "experiences of this type enrich our instructional curriculum and make the vocational school a better hall of learning." My father proudly saved the note, which had also been sent to the Gompers principal.

At the High School of Aviation Trades, his photo is not in the school yearbook and his name is not listed among the teachers. He is not mentioned by any students, although the yearbook devoted pages to jokes about their teachers, giving them gag legacies and making clear who was a favorite and who allowed them to catch up on sleep by showing boring films. Whatever my father did in his days at the School of Aviation Trades, it left him plenty of time and energy to lead the P.S. 61 PTA. And it did nothing to keep him out of trouble.

A few months later, there was another PTA celebration, now with the spotlight firmly and exclusively on my father, the sole guest of honor. The date was April 10, 1953. The occasion was a special victory banquet to mark the triumphs since January, which included both reversing the sale to the taxi company of the land earmarked for a new elementary school and finally getting the Board of Education to commit to a new building. Eventually, when construction was completed, P.S. 61 could emerge from shortened instructional days and maddeningly complicated class schedules. It was a triumph.

The photo in *Town & Village* on April 16 shows my father seated at the head table next to Robert F. Wagner, the Manhattan borough president. On Wagner's other side is my mother, Sylvia. The district congressman was also there, along with the state senator, the local assemblyman, and the city council representative. Superintendent of schools William Jansen sent a telegram of congratulations.

What was my father thinking as the master of ceremonies read aloud Jansen's words of praise and esteem? He smiled and thanked everyone for the leather briefcase presented by the PTA, but Jansen's praise for his service to the cause of education must have had a bitter taste. Four weeks earlier, on March 12, 1953, that same superintendent of schools had dictated a private letter of very different tone, ordering Saul to report for questioning to the Board of Education's assistant corporation counsel, the man in charge of the school system's anti-communist investigations.

CHAPTER 13

Hidden Records

Was my father the only teacher who was whipsawed between this sort of public praise and secret persecution? Were all the interviews conducted in those blacklist years as strange as the transcript I had read when I first discovered the hidden history of his teaching career? To find out more, I had to consult the special "anti-communist" archives of the New York City Board of Education. This turned out to be a complicated process, as arbitrary and secret as the original investigations.

The records of the Board of Education date from 1805, and they are vast. Within the sea of bylaws, directories, commissions, annual reports, and papers of individual officials, the Board of Education records of the Consolidated City of New York (1898–1970) is Subgroup E, and within that subgroup the records of anti-communist investigations are Sub-subgroup E11. This sub-subgroup occupies 71.5 cubic feet, which is the way librarians measure such collections. It is stored in 176 boxes. In 1975, all the records were moved from the Board of Education headquarters in Brooklyn to the Teachers College Library at Columbia University, in northern Manhattan. In 2003, they were transferred to the New York City Municipal Archives, where they now reside.

In most ways, this is an improvement. The Municipal Archives are housed in a grand nineteenth-century building in Lower Manhattan, just steps away from City Hall, the New York County Courthouse on Foley Square, and other municipal buildings. The archives' holdings include over a million photographs and almost as many maps, ledgers, and city directories, all available to the public. Here, ordinary citizens can explore records dating from the 1647 founding of New Amsterdam to recent births and deaths in all five boroughs. It is a triumph of public access to information.

The investigation of suspect teachers is a significant exception to this model of civic transparency. Documents from the Board of Education anti-communist investigations are remarkably hard to find and even harder to use. There are boxes and boxes of Board of Education archives, but the anti-communist files, as they are called, bear the following note: "This series of files contains materials the use of which must be restricted in order to preserve the privacy rights of individual teachers."

Those who want to consult these records must first explain the purpose of their research. An academic affiliation may speed approval, but even university-based scholars must submit signed and notarized forms promising not to reveal the identities of anyone who had been under investigation without express permission from the individuals or their heirs. As the forms state, violation of these terms carries the possibility of legal action. Once these forms are submitted, and after an additional in-person discussion of the rules, users are informed that they may take no photographs (now a common practice that saves hours of note-taking and reduces errors) and make no photocopies. The researcher's notes must be handwritten or typed on a personal computer. Without specific permission, documents relating to individual teachers must be paraphrased, not quoted, in any published work.

At first glance, this might seem like the restrictions that surround many kinds of archival research. It is common for researchers to have to leave personal possessions outside the reading room, using only pencil and paper provided by the institution to take notes. Computers are generally permitted, and often cameras, though photographs can be used only as research records; to publish an image of a document or other artifact requires additional and often costly permission. Some archives insist users wear special gloves before they can handle papers or photographs. Others limit the number of documents that can be seen at any given time. In England, Oxford's Bodleian Library is famous for making all users sign an oath swearing not to light a fire within the building.

The restrictions that surround the anti-communist archives of the New York City Board of Education are different, though. They are not about preserving the physical collection or maintaining a clear line of ownership but about keeping researchers from spreading the knowledge of what they have seen. In other archives, even in the case of well-known people who "seal" access to their papers for a period of years, there is generally a definite date when the seal will be broken and the contents made available without conditions beyond citation of the source. But at the Municipal Archives, there is no end date to the restrictions on the information. Like the teachers who were summoned for interviews at the Board of Education, the researchers who try to read those interviews are forced to make concessions before they even know what the conversation is about.

Why? Because of 9/11, or so I was told. There is no federal law guaranteeing the right to privacy after death, though there are laws regulating the rights of publicity that allow the estates of famous people to control the use of their works and images after death. Individual states, however, can make their own laws. After the attacks on the World Trade Center on September 11, 2001, news outlets tried to access telephone records for the final calls made by victims and families sued to block that access. In the March 24, 2005, ruling in *Matter of New York Times Company v. City of New York Fire Department*, the New York courts established the new legal principle that dead people and their families had a right to privacy. For how long? A "reasonable" time.

Although the ruling had nothing to do with the Board of Education files, it persuaded a judge in 2012 that the six or seven decades since the teacher investigations were not quite long enough to justify lifting the veil. A writer (and daughter of blacklisted teachers) sued for open access to the archives, but the judge in *Matter of Harbatkin v. New York City Department of Records and Information Services, et al.*, citing the 2005 case, ruled that unredacted files could be examined by scholars, but only with the restrictions I have just described. No one could be identified without permission. When Assistant Corporation Counsel Saul Moskoff was conducting investigations for the Board of Education in the 1950s, he routinely began his interviews promising that "there has been and will be no publicity given to the fact that you and I are having this discussion." Moskoff himself often violated his promise, proudly supplying reporters with names and addresses of teachers who were fired for refusing to cooperate, but the assurance of confidentiality still stood at the beginning of every transcript. In the words of the 2012 ruling, "Perhaps there will be a time when the promise made to [a teacher under investigation], and to others similarly situated, is so ancient that its enforcement would be pointless, but that time is not yet."

I have spent my life as a writer working in public and personal archives, from Library of Congress collections to the hatbox full of family papers hauled down from the top shelf of a closet, but I had never encountered restrictions like these. Even decades after the events recorded, the information inside those files came wrapped with a threat, a warning just as substantial as the woven tapes that tied the files closed.

In the explanation of its restrictions, the New York City Board of Records uses the phrase "out of an abundance of caution." The teachers under investigation in the 1950s are very likely dead, but apparently their children deserve protection. I was just one of many living descendants, after all. Those others, presumably, might object.

Would they? I doubted that the children of teachers forced out of the classroom thought they would inherit a taint of subversion, particularly since that subversion is never actually documented in the files. Children and grandchildren of teachers who became informers might have to revise their understanding of their ancestors, but they would not be personally harmed. The restrictions on the anti-communist files seem more a clumsy administrative ruling about protecting the city from liability than about preserving the reputations of people who were almost surely no longer alive. Like the original investigations, the permission forms are designed to chill the free exchange of information.

Since the question had already gone to court and I had neither the resources nor the stomach to reopen litigation, I found a notary and signed the forms. I asked my older brother Stephen and my younger brother Jonathan, born in 1953, for permission to quote our father's file. I decided not to try to hunt down the families of other teachers or reveal any names beyond those already identified in public documents. Then I made my way to the Municipal Archives, met with the apologetic and helpful archivist David Ment, and reaffirmed my willingness to abide by the rules. I chafed at the restrictions, but I wanted to see what those files contained.

Sitting at a battered library table in Lower Manhattan and examining the records of these investigations, I felt the past rush up to meet me in an assault of sensory memories. When I saw the ancient, brittle paper labels on the cover of each transcript, my throat filled with the bitter taste of glue, a memory from licking identical labels in the years before self-adhesive stickers. I was reminded of the quirks of manual typewriters, where a key might stick and type slightly above or below the line. I was whirled back to the clumsy way of copying documents by inserting carbon-coated sheets and thin translucent paper called onionskin behind the "original" piece of typing paper, all to be hit by the same typewriter keystroke, each copy blurrier than the one above it. I smelled the mustiness of old manila folders where secrets were stored.

As I began to read through the files, I was struck in a different but equally visceral way by the pettiness of the investigation. The issue at hand was always membership in suspect organizations and never about actual attempts to undermine the government. Many of the teachers being grilled had served in World War II, but the hill they were now being asked to die on was a single question, "Are you now or have you ever been a member of the Communist Party?" Even that question seemed performative. The answer didn't matter, because the very fact of being summoned presumed guilt, and any denial would be treated as a lie. Long-ago meetings, petitions, or youthful summer jobs were proof of dire intentions, as opinions were allowed to substitute for actions and then used to inflict humiliation, job loss, and public exposure.

There is a painful irony in reading these records. Along with the big question of party membership, most interrogations include attempts to get people to "name names," adding new suspects to the ever-growing list of undesirable teachers—but naming names was exactly what I had just promised not to do. I thought of all those possible descendants, innocent victims of their parents' travails, and how it had only now become so important to protect their privacy. Many of the teachers accused of disloyalty, subversion, and insubordination in the 1950s had young children. Nobody in the city administration was protecting those children when their parents were being hounded out of their jobs.

The record of what it was like to be a child of blacklisted parents is slim and depends on what those children have decided to reveal. Joan Wallach Scott, a prominent historian, recalled at her father Samuel Wallach's funeral that when she and her sister were children they had marched on picket lines carrying signs addressed to the superintendent of schools, William Jansen. "Dr. Jansen, You Had No Right to Fire My Daddy" one sign read. "My Daddy Is a Man of Courage. He Should Be Admired. Not Fired," read another. "We Read the Bill of Rights. Why Don't You?" was a third. None of this did anything to protect Wallach. In an interview for a film that was never completed, titled *Dreamers and Fighters*, Scott recalled, "In this period our lives were made richer by the cause that we fought for, but also more difficult—we paid for our beliefs and our parents' attempts to put them into action. The atmosphere was charged: veiled anxiety, deliberate cheerfulness."

Other children of the blacklists have their own painful stories. My childhood friend whose father lost his job soon vanished from my life, moving away because of her parents' divorce. Like me, she knew nothing about the blacklists but quite a lot about disrupted lives. Twelve-year-old Richard Flacks, whose mother and father were both fired for claiming their Fifth Amendment rights before the House Un-American Activities Committee, wrote a long and fervent letter to Dorothy Funn, who informed on his parents, asking how she could have done such a thing. Now in his eighties, Flacks still keeps the letters from his parents' students regretting their difficulties and mourning their absence from the classroom. One of the most poignant has a half-dollar coin taped to the note, a material token of sympathy and support.

Those young letter writers represent the other group of children far more harmed than protected by the blacklist purges: the students whose teachers vanished, often in midyear, because they retired, resigned, or were fired. There is no way to defend these sudden removals as improving education. Accusers and defenders alike often acknowledged that the people under suspicion were extremely talented teachers, though both the lead investigator and the superintendent of schools routinely asserted that talent and dedication were irrelevant. Like contemporary revisers of school curriculum intent on erasing the rough edges of historical truth, the red hunters of the 1950s deliberately deprived students of exposure to diverse opinions and approaches, trying to deny them the essential skill of evaluating information and forming independent judgment. The enormous loss to education, and to individual students, is invisible in the records.

Even with all the restrictions and omissions, I learned a lot going through the Board of Education anti-communist files. Within the context of individual interviews, I saw many acts of courage and quite a few of cowardice. I learned about personal grudges and the cruel disappointment of youthful loyalties that now seemed to have been misplaced. I also got to know the two men most active in the investigations: William Jansen, the superintendent of schools, and Saul Moskoff, the New York City Board of Education's chief interrogator.

CHAPTER 14

The Superintendent of Schools

Words like "workhorse," "solid," and even "stolid" attached themselves to William Jansen, a broad-shouldered pillar of calm in a turbulent city. In a cover story on October 19, 1953, *Time* magazine noted approvingly that "he was not a crusader, a scholar, or a showman." The *New York Times* emphasized "his understanding, his consideration of others and his kindness" in a profile on May 23, 1956. Historian David Caute, in his book *The Great Fear*, says Harold Cammer, a lawyer who defended many of the accused teachers, regarded Jansen as a "gentle, affable man who 'hated to do this' and who could on occasion be genuinely helpful." None of these accounts mentioned how active he was in rooting out possible communists in the city schools or how personally he embraced the task.

Six feet three inches tall, with a lantern jaw and carefully combed hair that had turned snowy white by the 1950s, Jansen presented himself as an impartial champion of education who stayed far above any political fray. Accounts of his career usually note his steady rise through the school system. He began as an elementary school teacher in 1910, became a junior high school principal in 1922, and started working in central administration in 1927, where he moved from promotion to promotion—mostly, it seems, by showing up and not causing problems. In 1947, after a long national search ended in the decision to go for someone noncontroversial, Jansen became New York City superintendent of schools. In an oral history interview after his retirement, Jansen insisted he was hired on his merit, citing everything from his Boy Scout awards (Silver Beaver, Silver Antelope, and Silver Buffalo,

William Jansen, New York City superintendent of schools from 1947 to 1958, during a difficult meeting. Credit: Municipal Archives, City of New York.

the highest accolade in scouting) to his appointment to the national principals' council. Other records show that he was a compromise choice. He held the job until 1958, when he turned seventy, the age of mandatory retirement.

However he got the job, William Jansen was a busy man. As head of the largest school system in the country, he oversaw 816 school buildings, many over fifty years old and constantly in need of repair. He oversaw curriculum and textbooks, summer classes, night schools, subsidized lunches, and a host of other responsibilities that allowed the city to fulfill its mandate to provide free public education for all. In the year I started kindergarten, Jansen supervised almost 42,000 teachers (day and evening), and over 9,000 other workers, from custodians and clerks to architects and elevator operators. He did not do all this alone. According to the *Official Directory of the Board of Education* for the academic year 1952–1953, the school system employed forty-eight assistant superintendents in charge of specific areas. But these assistant superintendents, and all the people under them, ultimately reported to Superintendent Jansen.

Close to a million students filled those schools. In planning for these children, Jansen seemed less concerned with their intellectual development than with making sure that each and every one of them was protected from any exposure to teachers or staff who might contaminate their minds with subversive ideas. Since contamination could take place through the mere presence of tainted people in the classroom, even if their teaching was entirely free of political content, Jansen felt that the only way to guard the tender youth entrusted to his care was to remove such people from the schools. When in doubt about whether a teacher was in fact a threat, or the process of removal legal, it was better to act swiftly and apologize later, if at all. Not that Jansen ever said this in public, but his private letters and correspondence tell the story.

Jansen viewed himself as a progressive educator, attuned to the needs of his students and acutely aware that many faced challenges at home that hampered them at school, but his view of liberals in general and communists in particular was entirely without nuance. To Jansen, any interest in communism was a total commitment. One could not be a little bit communistic any more than one could be a little bit pregnant, and even contact with a red-tinged magazine might plant the seed of subversion. He also believed that all communists, in any country, were secretly pledged to work solely for the Soviet regime, and so all must be rooted out of the schools.

How did he develop this conviction? In 1963, after his retirement, Jansen gave a series of interviews that became part of the Oral History

Archive at Columbia University, with the title *Reminiscences of William Jansen*. Jansen stipulated that the interviews were sealed during his lifetime and restricted after his death to "serious research scholars accredited for purposes of research by Columbia University"—another attempt to control information beyond the grave. Fortunately, I was able to meet his terms.

In his oral history, Jansen was not at all shy about taking credit for his pursuit of staff with alleged communist ties. He regarded the removal of several hundred teachers as "one of my main achievements." As he explained:

> A Communist is not fit to teach in our city schools where loyalty to our government, freedom of thinking, and high moral standards are some of the requirements of a good teacher. The Communist doesn't believe in academic freedom, although he yells about it; because with the Communist freedom means working within the Communist frame of reference. They don't believe in our morality because in 1937 in their manifesto they said that it's perfectly all right to lie if lying will produce the Communist result. Loyalty to our government— obviously that was not part of their belief because they believed, and the Communist doctrines time after time preached, such imperatives as "follow the Communist line," "work for the overthrow of the government" and so on.

Jansen also recalled that after he became superintendent of schools in 1947 it became "very obvious to me that we had a large number of communist teachers in our schools." The date is worth noting, since Jansen had been a special assistant to three superintendents before assuming the office himself, and by his own description he took care of all the "hot potato" assignments—including the investigation of Timothy Murphy for fascist activities and the counteraccusations that teachers at Gompers High School were communists.

What had happened in 1947 to suddenly show Jansen, after almost twenty years at the highest levels of New York City public school administration, that the schools were infiltrated by communist teachers? There are some likely triggers. It was an era of headline-grabbing events that doubtless made Jansen, like so many others, newly fearful of Soviet infiltration of American institutions. It was the time of Winston Churchill's 1946 declaration that an "iron curtain" of communist oppression was falling across Europe and of the New York City meeting of Hollywood producers that would soon lead to blacklists and the highly publicized trials of the "Hollywood Ten." There were the equally public hearings when journalist Whittaker Chambers accused Alger Hiss, a high-ranking employee in the State Department, of being a communist spy.

Jansen's thinking was also shaped by a much more local influence: politically powerful and deeply conservative New York City Catholics both outside and within the school system. Some historians have described the twentieth-century Catholic crusade against communism as the clash of two competing world visions, each international and each based on the premise of absolute obedience to central authority. While this is true in theory, it seems incomplete. Communism was never treated as an existential threat in countries far more uniformly Catholic than the United States. In Italy, for example, and in many nations in Latin America, it was entirely possible for an avowed communist to become an elected official while also being considered a good Catholic.

In the United States, however, Catholic immigrants from Ireland and Italy were still fighting their own battles against religious and social prejudice, and conservative Catholic activists within New York City saw the presence of left-leaning teachers as a dangerous menace—and possibly an opportunity to influence education. Twenty years earlier, Father Coughlin had reviled Jews as a menace to society, identifying them as communist agents. After World War II, with its revelation of Hitler's anti-Semitic atrocities, the new menace was called communism.

Catholic leaders were eager to discredit the public school system and to bolster parochial schools, but they also wanted to protect their influence in a public education system that employed many Catholic teachers and educated many Catholic students. One way to do this was to make sure one of their own onto the Board of Education.

George Timone, a lawyer and a prominent Catholic layman in his early forties, was a great favorite of the large and ultraconservative Brooklyn diocese. Less than a decade earlier, Timone had been involved in the pro-Nazi, anti-Semitic movements that swept through New York and the rest of the United States in the years just before World War II.

He had helped organize the fascist rally of the German American Bund at Madison Square Garden in 1939 and supported (but never officially joined) the Christian Front, another isolationist, pro-fascist, anti-Semitic group. Now, although he lacked any experience in teaching or school administration, he was the Catholic Church's favorite candidate for the New York City Board of Education, strongly promoted by Cardinal Spellman, head of the New York Catholic archdiocese and a firm believer that communist infiltration was a dire threat to the nation.

Timone joined the board in 1946, shortly before Jansen became superintendent of schools, and soon took steps to make sure "communists" and other subversive voices were kept out of the schools. One of Timone's first acts, urged by Cardinal Spellman, was to persuade Jansen to ban *The Nation* magazine from school libraries. This was just after *The Nation* carried an article that criticized the Catholic Church's power in the United States, starting with the influence of Catholic doctrine on the practice of obstetrics. Timone also managed to ban the popular historical novel *Citizen Tom Paine* from schools. Thomas Paine was a Revolutionary War hero best known for his fiery pamphlet *Common Sense*, but the 1943 historical novel was written by Howard Fast, a Jew and an acknowledged member of the Communist Party. Once again, powerful individuals with ultraconservative Catholic and anti-Semitic views were being used to police school libraries and control the tenor of public education, now under the guise of anti-communism.

Banning books was only the start of Timone's repressive attacks. In 1950, he successfully introduced what became known as the Timone Resolution, which barred the Teachers Union from operating within city schools or dealing with the Board of Education. This was a crippling restriction for a labor union.

By then, many teachers had moved to the rival Teachers Guild, established in 1935, but thousands still belonged to the original Teachers Union, an organization no longer allowed to advocate for its members to their bosses or in their place of work. One of those loyal members was my father. I can't know why he stayed with the union. Possibly because he liked his role writing for their newsletter, possibly because he thought by remaining in the Teachers Union he was standing up to oppressors, possibly because he was too busy to get around to the process of switching allegiances. And possibly, of course, because he was at least a communist sympathizer.

Along with its near ban on the Teachers Union, the Timone Resolution had several other elements that threatened teachers. One was that present membership in the Communist Party disqualified a person from working in the school system, while dismissal for past membership would be determined "by the particular facts and circumstances in that case." This sounded flexible but turned out to mean that informing on other teachers would be the only way to prove one had renounced past associations. Refusal to answer questions about past or present party membership would be regarded by the superintendent of schools and by the Board of Education as insubordination and, in the phrase carried over from the earlier Rapp-Coudert Committee, "conduct unbecoming a teacher."

William Jansen took the city's Timone Resolution to heart, along with the 1949 Feinberg law passed by the state legislature, which authorized the dismissal of teachers who could be linked in any way with a growing list of hundreds of organizations, events, and even periodicals that were deemed sympathetic to communism. When the House Un-American Activities Committee (HUAC) held hearings in New York City, the superintendent of schools told reporters that he believed any communist teacher should be immediately suspended. Jansen also was quoted as saying, "I'm convinced we have some Communists, but proof is difficult to obtain." That did not mean he would stop looking.

At the start of the 1949–1950 school year, Jansen publicly ordered all school principals to provide lists of teachers suspected of subversive leanings, as demonstrated by actions in or outside the classroom. Confronted by this enormous additional task on top of all their other responsibilities, almost all principals claimed there were no teachers to report, but Jansen continued to search. When a legal challenge to the Feinberg Law resulted in a temporary injunction on the state level, Jansen took advantage of a loophole that allowed local school boards to continue anti-communist investigations. A few months later, he was stirred into more open action. Like so much else in this sorry history of clashing worldviews, the deciding events occurred at the intersection of politics, money, and education.

CHAPTER 15

The Student Strike

Among the many strange items in my accordion file of mysterious souvenirs was a perforated sheet of six preprinted penny postcards, never mailed. The cards were all addressed to New York City mayor William O'Dwyer, and the message, with slight variations, was that teachers' real wages had declined from a decade before. All the senders had to do was sign the postcard and slip it in the mail. I had no idea what this was about or why these postcards had been saved. I had seen photos of my father demonstrating in Albany for higher wages, so I suspected union activity, but the story turned out to reach even further into the city schools.

O'Dwyer was mayor from 1946 to 1950, during which time there was a protracted three-sided salary war between the city's public school teachers, the mayor, and the governor of New York State. Teachers who had been released for military service during World War II were able to reclaim their jobs at their old schools and at their prewar salaries, but the cost of living had risen almost 70 percent during the war. Campaigning for reelection in 1949, O'Dwyer promised raises for teachers, but Republican governor Thomas E. Dewey (recently defeated by Truman in his bid for the presidency) instead pushed through a proposal that equalized salaries for all teachers at all levels. This had the effect of lowering pay for high school teachers, who previously were paid more than teachers in the lower grades. After the election, in early 1950, O'Dwyer eliminated funds for any raises from the city budget, though he did offer to give city teachers a one-time bonus of $200, less than

Dear Mr. Mayor:

Teachers' buying power is now 30% LESS than it was in 1939.

I urge you to adjust the salaries of all school employees.

RESTORE THE REAL WAGE OF 1939.

Respectfully yours,

....

115

....

THIS SIDE OF CARD IS FOR ADDRESS

HON. WILLIAM O'DWYER
Mayor of the City of New York
CITY HALL, NEW YORK

Dear Mr. Mayor:

Food and clothing prices have more than doubled in the past ten years. This has caused a sharp decline in the standard of living of school employees.

I urge you to adjust school salaries now.

RESTORE THE REAL WAGE OF 1939.

Respectfully yours,

....

116

....

Postcards urging teacher raises hint at the origins of a student protest for higher wages that spurred William Jansen to an ever greater search for subversive teachers. Credit: Collection of the author.

5 percent of their salaries. Meanwhile, school administrators received salary increases of 30 percent.

The postcards, like the frequent teacher rallies at the State Capitol in Albany and in front of New York's City Hall, were part of an ongoing struggle to get teachers the raises O'Dwyer had promised. The efforts were probably directed by the Teachers Union, though there seems to have been at least temporary cooperation with the rival union, the Teachers Guild. In any case, none of the protests and rallies worked. Whatever role my father had in the postcard campaign (Copywriter? Postcard distributor? Self-appointed preserver of the documentary record?), the salary dispute escalated in a way that solidified Jansen's determination to investigate suspect teachers.

The link between the postcards and the crackdown on teachers was a student strike. After O'Dwyer refused to raise salaries, teachers announced they would no longer supervise unpaid after-school activities like the yearbook or the *Gompers Echo*, two school publications where my father served as faculty sponsor. No orchestra, no newspaper, no stamp club, no school play. No baseball, basketball, cross-country, or any other sport. With their afternoons and evenings suddenly stripped of the extracurricular activities they loved, high school students across the city decided they wanted to support their teachers. Or, as Mayor O'Dwyer and Superintendent William Jansen saw it, they wanted to riot.

The student strike started on April 25, 1950, when 200 students at Brooklyn Technical High School, a selective public school located in Brooklyn's Fort Greene neighborhood, marched across the Manhattan Bridge to City Hall in Lower Manhattan, demanding higher pay for their teachers. Students and PTA supporters of pay raises noted that the mayor's salary had recently increased from $25,000 to $40,000 a year, while most teachers earned $5,000 a year or less. They were fighting for a raise of $600 a year.

The next day, 2,500 students from several Brooklyn high schools again marched on City Hall, and another 3,500 staged demonstrations at their schools, events that were covered by all the major newspapers of New York and Brooklyn. By April 27, the third day of protests, 20,000 students from almost every academic and vocational public school in Brooklyn were marching, with smaller delegations from schools in other boroughs. When police barricaded the footpaths of both the Manhattan and Williamsburg Bridges, blocking the pedestrian route across the East River, students jammed the subway to get to Lower Manhattan. Barriers were erected around City Hall, and a cordon of police, some on horseback, prevented the students from approaching. A sedan parked on nearby Pearl Street was overturned when students climbed on top, shouting they wanted more pay for their teachers and the restoration of sports and other extracurricular activities. There were reports of scuffles, and at least one firecracker, but the march was mostly peaceful, if spirited.

Mounted police and foot patrols broke up the demonstration, and the next day many fewer students came out to protest. School officials tried to distance themselves from the protest, denying that any students from their school had been among the marchers even though attendance records showed abnormally high absenteeism.

At this point the hunt for a scapegoat began. O'Dwyer refused to meet with the striking students, at the same time he was refusing to release evidence in a case alleging a police cover-up of mob-run organized gambling. The police corruption scandal was much more damaging and would soon persuade O'Dwyer to resign his office and accept an appointment as ambassador to Mexico, allegedly to avoid testifying. Nonetheless, the mayor did carve out time in his busy schedule to assign blame for the student strike. It was, he felt, the fault of their teachers, who had failed to fulfill what he told reporters was their "responsibility for molding children's character."

O'Dwyer was criticized for refusing to meet with protestors, but most of the blame was directed toward these unknown, unnamed radical teachers. The *New York Times* called it the most bitter controversy in the history of the world's largest school system. It also seemed important to the students. In the yearbook written two years later by seniors at Manhattan's High School of Aviation Trades, they listed the strike as the major activity of their sophomore year.

By April 30, 1950, the president of the Board of Education claimed that specific adults had encouraged the unruly students but refused to give their names. That same day, a front-page story in the *Times* estimated that forty thousand students were involved in demonstrations "that have kept the City Hall area and other parts of the city in turmoil for four days." For Jansen, the superintendent of schools, the strike was the spark that brought his anti-communist beliefs into the open. Teachers said they had nothing to do with the walkouts, but Jansen declared the student demonstrations the work of "subversive elements" who had infiltrated the schools. In memos now in the Municipal Archives, he demanded that police question students about teachers who had goaded them into striking. When police reported that students denied any such influence, Jansen refused to believe it.

Jansen's first move was to demand copies of the police reports on pupils apprehended for what was called malicious mischief. According to these reports, students were detained when they "threw [an] apple at [a] mounted patrolman" and "threw [a] rock at [a] mounted patrolman." Other infractions were "refusing to move," "resisting arrest," and "using abusive language." When the record showed that "none of the above five named boys indicated to police that they were urged by teachers to remain away from school," Jansen was unconvinced. He was sure that young people who questioned authority were being led astray by radical teachers.

It would take another year for teachers and the Board of Education to reach a salary compromise, and extracurricular activities resumed only in September 1951. Jansen's hunt for possible subversives working in the school system became public much sooner, just a week after the student strike. On May 8, 1950, Jansen suspended eight teachers, all active in the Teachers Union, without pay. It was the start of a new and highly publicized phase of the purge of New York City schools. Seven more teachers were soon fired for not cooperating with Jansen's investigation—these were the teachers who appealed their firing, an appeal that was rejected in a divided decision of the Supreme Court. It took twenty years for that decision, *Adler v. Board of Education*, to be overturned.

For eighteen months after these first firings, Jansen enthusiastically led the anti-communist campaign in his schools, including vigorous enforcement of recent New York State laws that would later be declared unconstitutional. He embraced the onerous and offensive Feinberg Law, which allowed him to fire any employee who associated in any way with anyone who advocated the overthrow of the American government—a category that stretched from communists and communist sympathizers to members of any groups identified as communists or socialist "fronts" by the shadowy compilers of dubious lists who flourished in this period. The suspect groups included several labor unions and multiple organizations working for world peace.

Jansen also eagerly acted on a 1950 New York State Supreme Court ruling that teachers who refused to answer questions from congressional committees could be automatically dismissed from the city's schools, though the ruling did not by any means require their firing. He routinely applied Section 903 of the city charter, a new amendment which banned city employees from invoking their Fifth Amendment right to remain silent during an official investigation. In *Slochower v. Board of Higher Education of New York City*, Section 903 was ruled a violation of due process, but that was not until 1956. By then, hundreds of teachers had been dismissed or felt compelled to resign or retire for insisting on their constitutional rights.

Board of Education records make clear that Jansen was not the detached administrator he was often described as being. For the rest of his tenure, he kept close tabs on his district's anti-communist investigations and those in other school districts across the country. He closely followed methods of the Senate's Permanent Sub-Committee on Investigations, led by Senator Joseph McCarthy, and HUAC. Teachers called to testify before government panels were automatically listed as alleged subversives in New York. Jansen also collected the names of people who signed petitions, wrote letters, or attended rallies protesting the dismissal of teachers; if they were teachers, he wanted them investigated. Letters and memos in the Board of Education's anti-communist files reveal that Jansen extended his pursuit of subversives to include those who might have slipped beyond the reach of his own investigations. He contacted police as far away as California to warn them that suspect former teachers might be trying to infiltrate their schools.

Jansen's richest source of information was the New York City Police Department's Bureau of Special Services and Investigations (BOSSI), also known as "the Red Squad." BOSSI had spent decades infiltrating what were labeled as radical groups, from immigrant community organizations to liberal-leaning summer camps, and it kept boxes full of index cards recording people they observed. Some of the names in these files were collected by police investigators like Mildred Blauvelt, a New York City detective who twice joined the Communist Party under different assumed names between1942 and 1951. Blauvelt gave HUAC names and addresses for some 450 party members, information that was shared with the Board of Education. Stephanie Horvath, another New York City policewoman assigned to BOSSI, did similar undercover work starting in 1942 until her public testimony against certain teachers and Department of Welfare workers in 1953. When Jansen began his anti-communist crusade, BOSSI records were added to his *Index File of suspected Communists and Subversive Organizations*, now also part the Board of Education Anticommunist Investigation Records at the New York Municipal Archives.

Attending party meetings was a sure way of being entered into BOSSI index files, but many very ordinary activities could also trigger the same special attention. My father's 1941 letters protesting the firing of Morris Schappes were neatly entered on an index card under his name. Other police reports consisted almost entirely of someone's suspicious appearance. "Wears a Van Dyke beard," one file notes as evidence of subversive tendencies. It took a strong presumption of prior guilt to construe this kind of information as proof of subversion—but that was Jansen's inclination. Other suspicious acts noted in the police files include signing a petition for a Liberal Party candidate to get on the city council ballot, watching a May Day parade, and sending a postcard to Branch Rickey, president and general manager of the Brooklyn Dodgers, questioning the absence of Negro players on his team.

This last evidence of "subversive" behavior reveals the sweep of the anti-communist searchlight. Branch Rickey is famous for breaking the color barrier in major league baseball by signing Jackie Robinson for the Dodgers in 1945 and supporting him and other Black players through the difficult and often hostile process of integrating professional baseball. For this and other pathbreaking achievements, Rickey was inducted into the Baseball Hall of Fame and received many other honors. He has been glowingly portrayed in at least three movies and one play, and his papers are in the Library of Congress.

The 1943 postcard from a Brooklyn high school teacher is never cited as possible inspiration for Rickey's courageous move two years later, but the card itself, like my father's 1941 letters, entered the police files and was used against the writer in a Board of Education investigation a decade later, by which time Jackie Robinson was well on his way to becoming a national hero. Apart from the perversity of citing such a message as evidence of un-American leanings, there is the chilling question of how the postcard ever made its way to the police. Was the post office screening Branch Rickey's mail? Was someone in his office working undercover for the police department? Did Rickey himself turn the postcard over to the authorities? I have not been able to find any answer to that mystery.

Meanwhile, my father, like the advocate for integrated baseball, was unaware of his entry into the index card files of subversive characters. The existence and long afterlife of that protest confirm that he was an active citizen. Also, he loved to write letters. He wrote to movie stars he admired and to starlets whose careers he thought would be helped if they followed his advice on getting more serious roles. He wrote to newspapers, whether to object to negative reviews of community theater productions, urge the opening of a second front during World War II, or comment on the heated emotions at PTA meetings. He wrote to thank the dry cleaner for his good service and to Eleanor Roosevelt to report on the success of his scout troop's paper drive. He seemed to be quite unconcerned by the possibility that anybody was monitoring his correspondence, though he did keep his reply from Mrs. Roosevelt and the autographed photos the movie stars sent back. As far as I know, this Hollywood fan mail did not enter his police file though stranger things certainly happened when Hollywood itself was under anti-communist investigation.

The police files were not Jansen's only source of suspects. No behavior seemed too small for his notice. When he spotted a newspaper article about three women who refused to answer the loyalty questions included on passport applications at the time, he sent a memo asking if they were by chance employed by the school system. If so, he ordered, they should be investigated. In one instance, he insisted on investigating a teacher who failed to participate in special school-based "homecoming" celebrations honoring then-controversial General Douglas MacArthur on his return to the United States. MacArthur had been fired by President Truman in 1951 for trying, without orders, to enlarge the Korean conflict into a full-scale war with communist China. Jansen himself had organized the celebrations. Such vigilance was wearing, and it took a lot of time. A year after the student strike and the expanded investigation of subversives in the schools, FBI director J. Edgar Hoover started a hush-hush operation, known as the Responsibilities Program, through which FBI agents shared Hoover's vast (and probably illegal) lists of teachers suspected of subversive associations at any time over the past thirty years, giving them to senators, governors, and top school officials. At this point, faced with the prospect of even more investigations, Jansen decided to ask for outside help. He requested an assistant from the city's legal office. He got a ratcatcher with a law degree.

CHAPTER 16

The Assistant Corporation Counsel

After Saul Moskoff took over the Board of Education anti-communist investigations in 1951, he became the chief architect of the crusade against subversive teachers in the New York City schools. It was Moskoff who drove my father and many of his colleagues out of teaching.

Moskoff was an attorney, not an educator. He worked for the New York City Law Department, which represents the city, the mayor, other elected officials, and the city's many agencies in all civil litigation. In press releases and news reports of his work, he was always identified as Assistant Corporation Counsel Saul Moskoff. Previously, he had defended city officials blamed for noxious smells coming from a Brooklyn garbage dump, investigated a business that was illegally telephoning race results to bookies from an office right next door to the headquarters of a special police rackets probe, prosecuted a crackdown on illegal pinball machines, and even represented the commissioner of public welfare in a paternity case. But for almost a decade, his sole job was to root out alleged communists from the city's public schools. He amassed his own lists of suspect employees, kindergarten through twelfth grade, and attempted to remove them from their jobs before they could contaminate young minds.

Moskoff's inquiries started with present or former members of the Communist Party of the United States of America, still completely legal before the much-disputed Communist Control Act of 1954. He quickly extended his net to include liberals of any party, reformers, activists, and, it seemed, anybody not in the school administration's good graces. By all reports, he relished the job.

John A. Dunne (*left*), chief investigator, and Saul Moskoff (*right*), assistant corporation counsel in charge of investigation of subversives in the school system, as they confer at pretrial session. Credit: *New York Daily News*.

Moskoff probably had another office somewhere else, but he conducted his Board of Education investigations from 131 Livingston Street in downtown Brooklyn. Designed by Charles C. B. Snyder in the early twentieth century as the main office of the Board of Education, this once-elegant building had later housed the Central Committee for the Junior Red Cross in 1942, when the Executive Secretary sent my father a letter of commendation for his work helping his summer school students gather books and games to send to army camps—another baffling document in my mystery file. By the 1950s, however, 131 Livingston was a storage facility for school furniture and other equipment that might someday be repaired. The building resembled the hideout of a comic book villain—a seldom-visited warehouse used as a secret lair to hide mysterious, ominous proceedings. Here Moskoff held his private interviews in a warren of small rooms on the fifth floor.

Teachers arriving for questioning rode an antique elevator past floors of broken school desks and battered file cabinets, then walked down a dim corridor before being ushered through a small anteroom and into Moskoff's office. Their accuser sat behind the sole desk in the room, with a chair for the teacher being questioned and another for a "teacher advocate" allowed to come along as advisor and witness, though none of the advocate's comments became part of the official record. Teachers were not allowed to bring lawyers, however. As the summons always noted, "the privilege of being accompanied by a teacher-adviser does not include the right to counsel at such interview."

Twenty-five years after the publication of *The Trial*, Franz Kafka's surreal exploration of persecution, Moskoff seemed to be reenacting it in real life. Interrogated by a lawyer in a quasi-legal proceeding, teachers did not know either the nature of the accusations against them or the identities of their accusers. Moskoff routinely denied that he used anonymous informants, which was not entirely true, but it hardly mattered, since he almost never divulged the sources of his accusations. In a few cases, teachers were able to prove that they had been confused with someone else, but they never had any way of refuting the accusations because they never knew exactly what they were.

Meanwhile, there was a great show of diligent recordkeeping. A stenographer took notes, and a tape recorder simultaneously chronicled the proceedings. Transcriptions of the recordings were checked against the stenographic record, typed, and placed between blue paper covers labeled on the front. Then they were filed away, covered in a shroud of secrecy that is still very hard to lift.

The very few photographs of Moskoff published during his career show a thin man with a long face, a sharp nose, and receding, wavy dark hair. Although he looked nothing like my father, Moskoff was in many ways his doppelgänger, another Saul born in Brooklyn only eight weeks later. Pondering the many similarities in their lives, I try to understand how they came to diverge so sharply in their ideas.

Both men attended large public high schools. Both were registered Democrats and supported their party's candidates. Both men served in World War II but neither saw combat or left New York State. My father fulfilled his army service at Pine Camp, a frigid outpost close to the Canadian border. Moskoff never even left home. He served in the

Fourth Regiment of the New York Guard, living in Queens and patrolling his Flushing neighborhood, showing up for training ten days in the summer and a scattering of weekends during the rest of the year. On at least one occasion, Moskoff joined other guard members in an exercise in which they traveled by bus and taxi to points around the city to test of their readiness to deal with concerted citywide sabotage by enemy agents. Other times, he participated in tactical training at the Wing Foot Country Club in Mamaroneck and in a simulated paratrooper invasion in Central Park. Moskoff's regiment was the same one that champion prize fighter Jack Dempsey joined with much fanfare in January 1942 and left, much more quietly, three months later. It was a soft post.

After the war, both Sauls returned to their former jobs, their wives and children, and their New York City apartments. Decades later, less than three years apart, they would be buried within two miles of each other in the acres of cemeteries on Long Island.

Beyond these coincidental similarities, there were other, more important traits the two men had in common. Both Sauls had a highly developed capacity for outrage, especially toward those who broke rules. Crucially, however, they interpreted those rules and enacted that outrage in very different ways. My father was a whistleblower, reporting school officials for financial, ethical, and professional transgressions that were eventually punished, but never without cost to his own career. He wrote letters, signed petitions, attended rallies, and went to protests. Moskoff, in contrast, was a stickler, a quibbler, and a maker of lists. He was a behind-the-scenes enforcer, determined to punish anyone who did not comply with the rules he was empowered to enforce, even if he could not prove them guilty of anything beyond the catchall accusations of "insubordination" or "conduct unbecoming a teacher," either of which was grounds for firing. Teachers who did not cooperate with Moskoff and did not either resign or retire after questioning were sent to Board of Education disciplinary hearings, which were public.

Both Sauls were Jewish, but Moskoff was far more observant; his appointment to work with Jansen was probably meant to serve as a rebuttal to the frequent and very plausible charge that the Board of Education was targeting Jewish teachers. Moskoff also considered himself something of a Talmudic scholar. He was proud of his knowledge of the Talmud, the primary authority on Jewish religious practice and belief, and became upset when teachers called in for investigation drew on their own religious education to challenge his interpretations. He was particularly offended when individual teachers said he was trying to make them behave like a *moser*, a Jew who informs on fellow Jews to the agents of the secular government. By Talmudic law, a Jew cannot do anything that would result in another Jew having to turn over financial or physical property to the government, a prohibition that could extend to depriving a fellow Jew of his means of earning a living.

Moskoff took these accusations seriously, particularly when they spread from 131 Livingston Street and into the public disciplinary hearings that sometimes followed. Although these hearings were not legal proceedings as such, both the prosecuting administrators and the supporters of the teachers routinely referred to them as trials. In 1953 Moskoff wrote to several rabbis, basically asking them to declare his operation kosher. "I am Assistant Corporation Counsel of the City of New York," he explained, "assigned to investigate the extent of infiltration by Communists into our school system and to institute disciplinary proceedings where the facts warrant it."

"Several trials are pending," he continued, "and I have reason to believe that Talmudic admonitions with respect to informers may be invoked in the forthcoming trials against certain teachers who are suspected of membership in the Communist Party. I would like your expert advice as to whether or not . . . the Talmudic law [can] properly be invoked by a person who has been asked: 'Are you now or have you ever been a member of the Communist Party?'"

Not every rabbi Moskoff approached responded, and even those who gave their blessings (so to speak) to his investigation reminded him that other rabbis might well disagree. What is most revealing is that Moskoff felt compelled to ask. The Board of Education investigations were entirely secular proceedings and did not have any legal status, though a formal trial in a court of law might follow in some instances. Teachers might plan a Talmudic defense, as some did, but there was no professional need for Moskoff to pay any attention. It seems that the judge Moskoff worried about was God.

Moskoff's spiritual scruples did not keep him from pursuing his quest for subversives or from turning his investigations into stylized dramas of sin and possible redemption, preferably through self-flagellation. What happened inside Moskoff's office was a ritual that began in assurances of confidentiality and proceeded quickly to unattributed accusations that could be erased only by "cooperating," which meant informing on others. Cooperators could return to ordinary life, although always with the ominous warning that they might be summoned again. Noncooperators saw their interviews end abruptly, the first step in a punitive process that ended in the termination of their teaching career in the New York City schools. If teachers continued to be "insubordinate," which included not just refusing to answer questions but also refusing to resign or retire from their jobs, Moskoff referred them for public disciplinary hearings before the Board of Education's trial examiner, Arthur Levitt. Here again, the Board of Education seemed careful to have Jews prosecuting Jews, to avoid charges of anti-Semitism.

Even in private, Moskoff's interviews followed the model provided by the vastly more publicized congressional loyalty hearings held around the country. These hearings were covered in minute detail by news outlets, particularly those where Hollywood writers and actors were forced to appear before grandstanding congressmen and a rapt throng of journalists and photographers who reported to the world.

Playwright Arthur Miller, learning in 1952 that writer Elia Kazan planned to name names to HUAC, immediately saw parallels to the seventeenth-century Salem witch trials, in which more than two hundred Massachusetts residents were accused of witchcraft over fifteen months, with twenty condemned to death. *The Crucible*, Miller's play set during the witch trials, opened on Broadway in January 1953, three months before my father was summoned to Moskoff's office. The play won the Tony Award for best drama of the year. Three years later, when Miller himself was called to testify before HUAC, he was terrified and enraged, though also amused, when, he claimed, the presiding congressman offered to dismiss his case if Miller would introduce him to his wife, actress Marilyn Monroe, and have her photographed shaking the committee chairman's hand.

The Crucible was immediately recognized as a barely veiled criticism of current events. Miller later wrote in his autobiography, *Timebends*, "The main point of the [HUAC] hearings, precisely as in seventeenth-century Salem, was that the accused make public confession, damn his confederates as well as his Devil master, and guarantee his sterling new allegiance by breaking disgusting old vows—whereupon he was let loose to rejoin the society of extremely decent people." Defense lawyer Harold Cammer told historian David Caute that he took Moskoff to see *The Crucible* to encourage him to reflect on what he was doing. The effort was "to no effect," Cammer recalled. "Moskoff could discern no resemblance between the Salem witch hunt and what had recently happened to New York teachers."

Even if he ignored the lessons of *The Crucible*, Moskoff's interviews in his hidden office followed the pattern Miller described. His standard opening was to tell the person before him, "the fact that you are here is held in the strictest of confidence and we propose to keep it that way. It is to your advantage as it is to ours." Moskoff would then summarize Board of Education policy, which established the framework of guilt by association on which Moskoff built most of his cases. He then proceeded with his own drama, with due concern for props and stage names. He was endlessly eager to be shown party membership books, which he seemed to believe were like bank books, with attendance records stamped at every meeting. He never saw one, but he always asked.

If a teacher admitted to having once been a member of the Communist Party (always in the context of confession, repentance, and informing on others), Moskoff asked for his or her party code name. Most of the cooperative teachers said they never had a code name, so Moskoff privately assigned them one himself, adding another layer of secrecy to his files. "Sugar" informed on my father, and so did "Falcon" and "Parachute." "Popeye," "President," "Spinach," "Wax," and "Sad Sack" informed on other teachers. These monikers sprang from Moskoff's imagination, possibly inspired by appearance, personal tics, or some other private association they triggered in his mind. The informers did not know they had been given these secret identities. The code names were for Moskoff's use, though it is not clear if they were meant to protect the informers or to fulfill his sense of what the dramatic occasion was due.

People who did not inform faced the double threat of loss of employment and public shaming. Moskoff promised confidentiality to teachers called in for questioning, but he apparently felt that promise could be withdrawn if those teachers went to disciplinary hearings or refused to answer questions from outside agencies like HUAC. In that case, Moskoff considered their treachery to be public knowledge. He was happy to provide names to reporters, as well as the names of the schools where they had worked and, often, their home addresses. As he boasted of how diligently he was protecting students and cleansing the schools, he was subjecting teachers and their families to hate mail and abusive telephone calls. That was of no importance, since he felt that those he judged guilty deserved whatever they got.

To Moskoff, the issue of guilt couldn't have been simpler. When he appeared at Board of Education public disciplinary hearings, Moskoff asserted that it didn't matter what teachers did or did not do in the classroom, because it was an established fact that communists had a "bounden duty" to indoctrinate all with whom they came into contact. Using the language he often employed, Moskoff argued that "proof of membership in the Communist Party is proof of inclination and proof of the status of an individual as a teacher is proof of opportunity."

Moskoff's reasoning was presented like a logical demonstration, but it was profoundly flawed, based on false assumptions about political parties, teaching, and the whole vast enigma of human behavior. It did irreparable harm to the entire system of education. With his single-minded focus on the question of communism, Moskoff ignored the real possibility that he was helping to foster totalitarianism under a different name.

Moskoff also had set speeches for his private interviews, memorized over long months of practice. His presentation was polished and well rehearsed. After his opening salvo, the rote assurance of confidentiality that became the justification for restrictions many decades later, and his summary of the Timone Resolution (though George Timone was never mentioned by name), Moskoff declared that present membership in the Communist Party "constituted a basis for disqualification from continued employment in the school system." Past membership, while not in itself an immediate basis for dismissal, required an investigation, since "there was a relationship between past membership and present fitness to teach." Furthermore, Moskoff noted, the resolution obliged the superintendent to question teachers about present or past membership in the Communist Party, and it obliged teachers to answer truthfully. Refusal to answer questions would be regarded as insubordination and conduct unbecoming a teacher. This double threat became so familiar that children of teachers in the 1950s can still rattle the phrases off in conversation today.

If a teacher asked for a second interview and seemed ready to name names, Moskoff had another speech he used, emphasizing how painful the process was for both of them. "It is distasteful to me and it is probably distasteful to you, but recognizing the obligation that is placed upon me and which I think rests upon you as a teacher and as a citizen, I am constrained to ask you certain questions." This was usually followed by an assurance that Moskoff's aim was not to pursue people who had recognized their errors and left the Communist Party but only those who persisted, "in face of all the facts and developments," with membership in the party or allied organizations—like the Teachers Union. After these set speeches, Moskoff would typically pull out a list of names, asking the teacher which ones he or she recognized as subversives. No new information needed to be volunteered, only a confirmation of what it seemed Moskoff already knew.

Theatrical gestures marked both sides of Moskoff's secret interviews, with cooperators and noncooperators alike. Months of highly publicized Senate and House hearings about "un-American activities" had made everyone familiar with investigators' refusals to provide evidence for their accusations or listen to rebuttals from the defense. Indeed, defense attorneys were often jailed for contempt if they tried to argue their cases. This was known to anyone who followed news reports of congressional anti-communist hearings or Board of Education trials.

Nonetheless, those who came into Moskoff's chamber often appeared with prepared statements defending their patriotism, which they were eager to read aloud and have included in the record. Sometimes they prostrated themselves before the inquisitor in their haste to repent for past offenses, with an explanation of how their youthful selves had strayed. Sometimes they offered carefully researched defenses of civil liberties. Some teachers provided long explanations of why communism seemed attractive during the hard times of the Depression and before the exposure of Joseph Stalin's brutalities.

The transcripts of these interviews suggest that the investigator and his suspects inhabited separate and very different intellectual and moral worlds. Many of the teachers called into Moskoff's office came armed with testimonial letters of their excellent record as teachers. They appealed to the Constitution and the Bill of Rights and gave Moskoff carefully written capsule histories of the 1930s and early 1940s. These documents were meant to explain why communist ties once seemed both innocent and hopeful. I am not permitted to reveal the names of the people who composed these histories, but I can attest to the palpable anguish behind their words.

None of these statements was ever considered relevant. The teachers wanted to explain democracy. Moskoff wanted yes or no answers. The issue for the investigator was twofold, and very simple:

Are you now or have you ever been a member of the Communist Party?

Are you willing to prove your loyalty by implicating others?

Teachers hoping to clear themselves by turning in other possible communists—the famous "naming names"—were not Moskoff's only source of suspects. The Rapp-Coudert Committee had interviewed and interrogated hundreds of people in the New York City academic world before 1942, and its files were kept and shared for many years with school officials. FBI lists of suspect characters, dating as far back as the 1920s, were also starting to be shared. These lists were easily cross-referenced with the names of teachers.

As Jansen had done before him, Moskoff also used police lists of members of leftist organizations, people who attended public meetings like the Scientific and Cultural Conference for World Peace (held at New York's Waldorf Astoria hotel in March 1949 and given major coverage in local newspapers and national magazines), subscription lists of suspect periodicals like the *Daily Worker*, and random accusations, often unsigned, that came in the mail.

Moskoff's files were well stocked with what, in another time and place, would have been dismissed as the suppositions of cranks and lunatics. Many letters he received, signed and unsigned, referred to professional grudges or family quarrels, suggesting that the anticommunist hysteria of the 1950s became a license to exact personal revenge or exercise private prejudices. How tempting it must have been to pin the label of subversive on a co-worker, neighbor, or relative you didn't like—and how easy, when people in authority happily accepted anonymous accusations without any supporting evidence. Here is a typical letter from 1952. It is handwritten, unsigned, and full of venom:

> In line with the present investigation of Red Schoolteachers I would recommend that [name of a teacher] be asked point blank if he is a Commie, my guess is that he will admit it. . . .
> He condemned all newspapers as liars except the Daily Worker but enjoys under our American System about $7,000 a year as a school teacher in two sessions. Why? He prefers the regimentation of Red Russia to American Freedom.
> I will not sign this letter but if I read of his being questioned will come forward with more information.
> I do not know if he has membership in any other Commy [sic] Societies.

Another letter spoke of a dangerously liberal relative who had received a promotion. "Something should be done about protecting our children from these destructive influences," the writer warned. "Many of them are working their way up the ladder to higher positions. They should be stopped before it is too late." Since this letter was signed, the writer got a call from Moskoff asking for further information.

As these letters indicate, the Board of Education Anticommunist Investigation Records hold much more than the transcripts of Moskoff's interviews with allegedly subversive teachers, voluminous though they are. The records also show how he compiled his lists of suspects and how he shared information with the public.

One of the things he liked to do was tabulate his investigations, creating scorecards of teachers summoned for questioning and then expelled from the classroom. Newspapers were happy to publish Moskoff's tallies. His appointment was heralded in a slangy *Brooklyn Daily Eagle* column on June 25, 1951: "The Board of Education is prepping a new war on Communist teachers, with Asst. Corp. Counsel Saul

Moskoff leading the fireworks." *The Tablet*, a conservative weekly newspaper that was the unofficial mouthpiece of Brooklyn's Roman Catholic Diocese, zealously reported on Moskoff's work, reinforcing the common impression among liberals that the Catholic Church was actively involved in the purging of Jewish teachers. Among the big New York metropolitan newspapers, the *New York Daily News* covered Moskoff frequently (far more often than either the *New York Times* or the *New York Herald Tribune*), with the same distinctive style it deployed for the gangland killings and Hollywood scandals that so often appeared on its pages.

Every few months, Moskoff released his latest figures to wire services that spread his reports to newspapers across the country and around the world. On October 4, 1952, he told a reporter from the *Chicago Tribune* that in the last eighteen months, ninety-one teachers "with alleged Communist Party ties had been dismissed or forced to leave city employment." By November, there were 193 pending probes. On May 5, 1953, Moskoff was happy to announce he had thirty teachers and clerical employees scheduled for interviews over the next several weeks, with one hundred others already under preliminary investigation. One of them was my father.

CHAPTER 17

The Interview

On April 27, 1953, seventeen days after the Victory Banquet celebrating my father's leadership in wresting approval for a badly needed new school from a reluctant Board of Education, he reported to Saul Moskoff's office at 131 Livingston Street. He had rescheduled twice, stalling for time as he searched for a teacher advocate who would assist him at the interview. After the last rescheduling, Moskoff wrote that any further delays would be considered insubordination and grounds for immediate firing.

David Flacks, who finally agreed to accompany my father, was a longtime editor of *Teacher News*, the union newspaper to which my father contributed, as well as an elementary school teacher at Brooklyn's P.S. 174. Flacks was a popular teacher and renowned for the witty satirical songs he composed for union events. His wife Mildred had already been fired for refusing to name names before a HUAC committee, and Flacks would soon follow her out of the classroom for similarly citing his Fifth Amendment rights. While he was still employed, Flacks served as a teacher advocate multiple times, although nothing he said is recorded in Moskoff's files.

Like so many others, before and after, the two men made their way up to the fifth floor, past the rooms of furniture waiting for repair, through the anteroom where a typist sat transcribing the recordings of previous interviews, and into the inner sanctum. Maybe my father came confidently. The record suggests that he did have a plan.

My father was not stupid. The former chairman of his department had already resigned. Another colleague at Gompers High School,

SAMUEL GOMPERS VOCATIONAL HIGH SCHOOL

Date February 3, 1948

OFFICE OF THE PRINCIPAL   (Copy to Mr. Waldt)

TO: Mr. Schur

SUBJECT:

Thank you for the "second" issue of the "The Echo". The idea of having
a "welcome" issue is an excellent one.

I should also add that I am very well pleased with the initative and
...played and the results secured during the past term

OFFICE OF CIVILIAN DEFENSE

Washington, D. C.

November 4, 1941

Mr. Saul Schur
C Department of English
Samuel Gompers Vocational Hi,
Southern Boulevard at 145th :
The Bronx
New York, New York

Dear Mr. Schur:

    Mrs. Roosevelt has refer
October 27 to me for reply.

    She asked me to tell you
the program of your students is
your initiative and imagination
your own community, and the comm
Defense is vital.

    The Office of Civilian Def
augurate national programs because
are so different. I shall, howeve
out to other schools and groups th
students are rendering.

    Sincerely yo

Jane Seaver, Youth Member
Volunteer Participation Committee

This is to Certify that

Saul Schur

HAS DULY QUALIFIED AND IS REGISTERED WITH THE
BOY SCOUTS OF AMERICA
FOR ONE YEAR AS

Chairman
Pack 2
Bronx, N.Y.

IN ACCORDANCE WITH THE CONSTITUTION AND BY-
LAWS OF THE BOY SCOUTS OF AMERICA
IN WITNESS WHEREOF ITS SEAL IS HERETO AFFIXED

DATED April 30, 1940

CHARACTER - CITIZENSHIP

Saul brought these and other proofs of his outstanding record as a teacher and
citizen when he was called for an interview about his alleged subversive activities.
Credit: Collection of the author.

Arthur Newman, had been suspended in January 1952 after refusing to answer Moskoff's questions about Communist Party ties. Newman's public Board of Education trial had taken place the previous October, after which he was fired for "insubordination." My older brother recalls Newman as a gentle man who visited our apartment and encouraged our father not to be intimidated. Edward N. Wallen, the current Gompers High School principal, had spoken in Newman's defense before the Board of Education, to no avail. Nonetheless, Saul brought letters of praise from Wallen to present at his own interview, mostly referring to his work establishing a student newspaper and making students in "the Annex" feel connected to their school.

My father brought other testimonials. As I looked at the copies of these documents in the Board of Education's restricted files, I recognized most of them from the originals in the mysterious collection of papers I found after my parents died. What my father and mother had saved for decades were the flimsy props Saul had brought to buoy up his character and protect his job against a surging wave of political suppression: his card as a Boy Scout troop leader; his honorable discharge from the army and his military certificate of good conduct; the article from *Town & Village* about the Victory Banquet in his honor; and a prewar letter from a member of the Board of Education congratulating him on his courage in being willing to testify about abuses at Gompers High School. There was also the wartime letter from First Lady Eleanor Roosevelt's office praising his efforts at organizing students in a paper drive. Moskoff took the copies of testimonials my father presented and put them in his file, where they would be joined by the typed transcript of their conversation.

There are scores of these transcripts in the Municipal Archives, each in its own blue folder, but this was my own father under fire. I had read the transcript when I first ordered a copy, but here amid the stacks of other folders, each an attack on a single teacher's life, I felt more than ever that I was being schooled in defiance and despair.

After a brief discussion of the role of the teacher advocate, Moskoff began with his usual speech. "The fact that you are here, Mr. Schur, is held in the strictest of confidence and we propose to keep it that way. It is to your advantage as it is to ours." Following his customary summary of the Timone Resolution, Moskoff prepared to move on to his real interest: "Are you now or have you ever been a member of the Communist Party?"

Before he could ask, however, the interview took a turn quite different from any of the others I had read. My father interrupted Moskoff with a question of his own. He wanted to know if the Board of Education's resolution applied only to alleged membership in the Communist Party. Or did it also apply to other subversive activities in the schools as well?

"Would you probe into evidence of subversive activities if I were to present it with reasonable proof of teachers who are now in the school system, or Superintendents, or past Superintendents?" my father asked. This was an important point, he felt, because when he had brought in evidence of Nazi Bund activities in the schools, he had been told that such activities warranted dismissal only if they happened in the classroom.

It was a novel defense—not that he was innocent or guilty, but that the board had already decided in his favor, as shown by the official insistence twelve years before that the Board of Education could not and would not discipline teachers for activities outside the classroom. He wanted to know if Moskoff was ready to reopen an investigation of past subversion in the schools.

Moskoff demurred. "Well, if I am confronted with any evidence indicating that any person is a member of any group—a Fascist or Communist group—advocating the destruction, so to speak, of democracy, why then I should certainly do everything within my power to determine what the facts are and if the facts warranted charges, to recommend charges. You see, my function here is to determine what the facts are." Then he tried to return to his standard opening question.

Again, my father interrupted, offering to bring evidence to show fascist infiltration of the schools. Moskoff was determined not to be diverted. "Supposing we hold that off for a few minutes to continue our discussion," he responded, before continuing, "Now I ask you: Are you now a member of the Communist Party?"

My father was equally determined. "Well, on any questions—that I want to make clear, regardless of what you have said—that any question that deals with political beliefs, anything connected with anything outside of the school system, I feel that is an improper question," he insisted.

Moskoff replied, "The Board doesn't quite agree with you, Mr. Schur," and went on to elaborate. "The Board feels that a person who was or is, rather, a member of the Communist Party, which, in the opinion of the Board, based upon certain developments, is an organization which was devoted to the overthrow and is devoted to the overthrow of the government by force and violence, and which is a subsidiary, so to speak, of a foreign power—the Board feels that membership in such an organization does have a relationship to the competency of a teacher."

Now my father brought out his central grievance, and his real claim of irregularities in the current investigations. "We asked the same question of Mr. Timothy Murphy in the presence of the Board of Superintendents. The member of the Board of Education who asked the question was ruled out of order on the basis that it must only be a question relating to [Murphy's] classroom activity."

Moskoff liked to debate, and this was a challenge he could not resist. What if a teacher was a member of the Ku Klux Klan, he asked, advocating violence against the Negro, against the Catholic, and against the Jew? My father answered that the Board of Education ruled that such membership was outside their jurisdiction if it did not enter the classroom.

"Well, I am asking you, is that what you think?"

Saul stayed with his original argument, that any evidence not pertinent in the Murphy investigation was not pertinent now. Therefore, the superintendent of schools had no right to inquire about a teacher's activities outside of school.

Then the interview took another twist, as my father described how he and other teachers had been called to the Board of Education headquarters for reporting on Murphy. "We were up on the carpet. We were told that we would eventually be fired from the school system" for calling attention to what the teachers felt was clearly subversive behavior by a fellow teacher. "That was twelve years ago," he added. "Believe me, this is something that has been on my mind for many years."

Moskoff could not believe what was happening. "Mr. Schur," he sputtered, "let's not divert this—this is an inquiry by me at which I had hoped to put questions to you and get answers to them. It is not an inquiry by you of me or the Board of Education."

Then my father brought the conversation up to the present. "Dr. Jansen was involved in all this," he said, "although he played a very silent role at the time. He was not a man to express an opinion either way."

"There is no point in carrying this on," Moskoff exclaimed, before asking yet again if my father was "at the present moment a member of the Communist Party."

Once again, my father didn't answer, insisting that it was not a proper question, particularly since a case was currently being adjudicated in the courts on the legality of such probes. "This is a very important issue," he added, "and it can lead to very serious harm in the school system once we begin this kind of thing. I think already it has done tremendous harm."

So much had happened to Saul since Murphy's anti-Semitic outburst on the school playground: a global war; three years in the army; two children and another on the way; a triumphant role leading his local PTA in a successful campaign for new building construction. And yet my father's outrage was as fresh as it had been twelve years before. Whatever Moskoff might ask, my father wanted to talk about the way he and the other teachers filing complaints had been treated during the Murphy case. He had been ignored, dismissed, and then called out of his classroom to be told his righteous exposure of evil could cost him his job. It had been weighing on his mind ever since, and he was determined to be heard.

Moskoff was equally determined not to listen. In referring to school policies of 1941, my father might as well have been invoking legal codes of ancient Mesopotamia. Moskoff returned again to the question of whether my father was or ever had been a member of the Communist Party. He added a further threat. "I again tell you that your conduct might well be regarded as insubordination and conduct unbecoming a teacher, and in the face of that admonition, do you want to amplify your answer any more than you have already given?"

Yes, my father did, though not in the way Moskoff hoped. He presented a justification for a life dedicated to education:

> Here is who I am. This is what bothers me: I have worked very hard for the schools, I really have, and I have stuck my neck out because you know what it means when a teacher leads a parents' association

and fights for a school, and when Mr. Pigott says "You don't need a school"—when I happen to be in the uncomfortable position of having to prove that his figures are false, nevertheless we won the school and I fought for it . . . so here you put me in a very uncomfortable position that I am being questioned and I can tell you very frankly, and I am not making this as a threat or anything . . . but the fact that this is a reprisal because I know that Mr. Pigott has told the parents that he is going to get—

Now it was Moskoff's turn to interrupt, reverting to his usual pat speech.

"Mr. Schur, don't put me in the position of having to put on the record the basis for having called you in. I think it is as much to your advantage as it is to mine to rule that out, so don't question the reasonableness of my having called you for inquiry because I will then have to put on the record the basis for it and I don't think it will be to your advantage, so let's not go into that."

"I don't know what the advantage or disadvantage is," my father retorted. "I am not a lawyer, but all I know is when a member of the Board of Superintendents threatens to get the person responsible for publicizing the errors that he made and tells the parents' association, which I am not affiliated with, and makes remarks like that, what am I to feel? Obviously somebody has looked to see if they can get me for something."

Saul believed he had been summoned to Moskoff's office because of his successful leadership in getting the Board of Education to build a new school—the occasion of the recent Victory Banquet. More directly, he thought the summons was retaliation for his successful exposure of what seemed like a scheme to take land designated for a new school and sell it to the Yellow Cab Company. He said he had evidence that George F. Pigott Jr., the assistant superintendent of housing, the man responsible for construction and maintenance of all the city's schools, had publicly threatened revenge for my father's exposure of what might have been willful distortions of data.

Moskoff dismissed the accusation, saying his investigation had nothing to do with Pigott, which was probably true. But it was also true that my father and Pigott had been on opposite sides of other memorable disputes that stretched back to those contentious years before the war.

Before he was assistant superintendent of housing, Pigott had been in charge of what was then the new field of vocational education. It was Pigott who oversaw the planning for Gompers Vocational High School, where my father worked, and all the city's other schools that trained students for careers ranging from printing to dressmaking to electrical engineering. Pigott may have been responsible for the first crisis at Gompers, before it even opened, when the decision not to hire union electricians—at a school dedicated to "the electrical arts" and named after the founding president of the American Federation of Labor—led to a protest that halted work not only at Gompers but at all schools across the city. Pigott knew about the investigation of the principal at Gompers who had padded enrollments to increase his pension. He would have been familiar with the charges against Timothy Murphy, including the racist, anti-Semitic, and anti-Italian behavior at Gompers Vocational High School, Murphy's undue violence in disciplining students, and the evidence that Murphy was diverting funds meant for outstanding students to support pro-fascist activities. Any of these would seem clear evidence of "conduct unbecoming to a teacher." And yet, in spite of Murphy's eventual censure, when he was removed from Gompers he was transferred to a different school where he was given a raise for teaching in the newly formed War Industries Training Program. The director of that program? George Pigott.

When Moskoff said he was not at all interested in land sales, my father expressed what seems like genuine surprise. The battle for new schools was very fresh in his mind. Once again, it seemed to him, he was being punished for being a whistleblower.

Moskoff insisted the interview had nothing to do with Piggott, but my father didn't believe him.

"Mr. Schur," Moskoff repeated, "let me tell you right here and now, I have no interest."

"No," my father said, "but somebody else does."

This was an unacceptable challenge to Moskoff's independence. "No one else has [an interest in calling you here]," he insisted, "because nobody directed me to call you in. Nobody knows who I am going to call in. I called you only because I obtained certain information concerning some activities of yours and these activities do not relate to [current] problems in the schools about which you have spoken, so let there be no question about that."

"There's a strong question in my mind," my father insisted. "The fact that I was designated 'The Man of the Year' for the Stuyvesant Town Community, the work that I have done for the community, I feel it is an important thing."

Saul was on a roll. He read aloud his citations as Man of the Year, his commendations from the district superintendent, his congratulations from the Manhattan borough president for the excellent way he had worked for the schools. More tributes followed, including, finally, the 1941 letter of commendation from Eleanor Roosevelt.

"What was the date of that letter?" Moskoff asked, suddenly alert. He then followed with several more questions about exactly when my father started the wastepaper campaign of which he was so proud, and when in 1941 he started working with the Junior Red Cross. Finally, Moskoff felt able to circle back to his real question.

"Would you tell me at the time you got that letter whether or not you were a member of the Communist Party?"

"Oh, come on—" my father exclaimed, astonished. When Moskoff asked again, my father repeated that he was still very upset about the betrayals of the Murphy case and the threatened reprisal from Piggott.

"You say this has nothing to do with an anonymous letter?" he asked.

"No, sir," Moskoff answered.

"Or even people writing in letters stating so-and-so expressed such an opinion?"

"No, it does not."

Eager to regain control of the conversation, Moskoff reluctantly revealed the source who had triggered my father's interview. An informant Moskoff had code-named "Sugar" stated he "has a definite recollection" of my father hosting meetings of communist teachers at some unspecified, long-ago date.

My father was incredulous. "At my home?" he asked.

Yes, Moskoff answered.

"At my home?" my father asked again.

Moskoff's files were cross-referenced by the code names he had given informants. I am not permitted to divulge who "Sugar" was or what he said, but I was able to read his interview. What I know—what my father could never learn—is that the "definite recollection" came only after considerable prodding from Moskoff, including a direct mention of my father's name and the blunt question, "What about him?"

Sugar was unusual in that he had volunteered to speak to Moskoff, making an appointment, he said, to clear his conscience. The main blot on Sugar's record, as he saw it, was a job he had held during the early summers of his career. Like many teachers, he had earned extra money working at summer camps, and he was now worried that his youthful jobs at places that promoted brotherhood and hired performers like Pete Seeger might now taint his reputation.

Moskoff had questioned Sugar at length about summer camp activities twenty years before. He asked if campers were taught to sing the communist anthem, "The Internationale," and he was clearly disappointed to learn they had not. Like the code names and membership books, the anthem figured large in Moskoff's dramatic imagination. But Sugar did remember another detail of the prewar years. There had been a group of teachers, he said, all living in the Parkchester housing complex in the Bronx around 1940, who met to discuss politics. Moskoff suggested several names, then asked if Sugar could recall any other members of the group. "What about Saul Schur?" he asked.

I have no idea why at this moment Moskoff brought up my father's name. His memory thus forcibly refreshed, Sugar agreed that some of the meetings had been at my parents' home and even said Saul was an organizer of the group, "the kingpin, as it were," a description Moskoff repeated back to my father. As for the assertion that the teachers were communists, that is not in Sugar's testimony.

After citing the revelation from Sugar, Moskoff pressed on with his questioning. If Saul, like Sugar, had decided to keep his job by identifying possible communist teachers, he might have gotten the code name "Kingpin." But that was not my father's intention. One of the many vicious snares of these interrogations was that teachers who admitted communist ties were immediately fired, while teachers who denied it were assumed to be lying—and were fired for refusing to state the truth. Instead of engaging with Moskoff's carefully constructed script, Saul met each question with a statement that turned the interview in a different direction.

When asked again if he was or had ever been a member of the Communist Party, my father again brought up his telegram from Superintendent Jansen, the newspaper clippings about the Victory Banquet, the many other ways he had been honored for service to his community, and his long and exemplary record as a teacher. As to whether or not he had been a member of the Communist Party in 1941, my father kept on reminding Moskoff that in 1941 the Board of Education had ruled that outside activities were irrelevant to school investigation and that any changes to that position were currently being adjudicated in court.

The conversation circled around and around, a dance of insistence and resistance. When asked yet again if he had ever hosted or attended meetings of teachers who were communists, my father said that he would discuss nothing that happened outside the classroom. It was dangerous to admit to anything, he said, no matter how innocent. Given the possibility of misinterpretation, even the most ordinary acts might be taken as proof of association with suspect groups. "I wouldn't even sign my daughter's report card," my father said. At that point Moskoff declared the interview over, but it was not the end of the case.

CHAPTER 18

Informers

As he frequently did, Moskoff turned to other sources to confirm his suspicions about my father. He had already sent an investigator to our apartment to pressure my father to confess his communist ties. That had brought no results and neither had the formal interview at Moskoff's office. A week after that frustrating interview, Moskoff sent another investigator to confront my father at work, which was now the High School of Aviation Trades. Once again, the key question was, "Are you now or have you ever been a member of the Communist Party?" Once again, my father refused to answer. But he was deeply shaken. "What am I going to do?" he asked his brother-in-law right after his interview with Moskoff. "How am I going to tell your sister? How am I going to get another job?"

Saul would have been even more fearful if he had known he was about to be swept up by a whirlwind named Bella Dodd.

Bella Dodd—her full name was Maria Assunta Isabella Visono Dodd—was born in Italy in 1904, the last of her mother's ten children, but came to New York when she was six. A trolley accident that led to the amputation of her left foot did not slow Dodd down in any way. After graduating from high school and Hunter College, the all-female branch of the City University, she taught at Hunter from 1926 to 1938 while also getting a master's degree from Columbia University and a law degree from New York University. In 1930 she traveled back to Italy, where she was appalled by what she saw of Italian fascism. That trip was also where she met her husband, the American John Dodd, and fell in with a crowd of activist teachers and labor

In 1955, Lawrence Martin of the *Denver Post* reported on the shadowy accusations hounding teachers across the nation, and especially in New York City. Credit: Collection of the author.

union members on the boat returning to New York. These were the only people, she thought, who were working against fascism. In 1938 she quit her low-paying job at Hunter for an even lower salary as the legislative director at the Teachers Union, fighting for legal protections for teachers. "Firebrand" is the word most often used to describe her in these years.

By the late 1940s, Dodd's life had taken a downward turn. Separated from her husband, no longer teaching, and expelled from the Communist Party of the United States of America (CPUSA), which was riven by fighting factions, this restless and disillusioned woman of enormous energy and talent came under the spell of Fulton J. Sheen. Sheen was a charismatic and ambitious Catholic priest who hosted popular programs on the radio and later on television, explaining Catholicism and using these modern media pulpits to advance his religious and political priorities. Fighting communism and bringing converts into the Catholic Church were the central tenets of his chosen mission. Sheen had already converted several former Communist Party members and journalist Clare Booth Luce (wife of magazine magnate Henry Luce) when Dodd was introduced to him. This was in Washington, D.C., where he served as a parish priest while teaching at Catholic University.

In 1951, Sheen was appointed auxiliary bishop of the Archdiocese of New York, where Dodd then lived. Born Catholic, Dodd had renounced the church during her years with the Communist Party. Now she embarked on weekly religious instruction with Sheen, and after a year she was readmitted to the Catholic Church in a private ceremony in New York City's Saint Patrick's Cathedral. A few months later, after announcing her conversion, Dodd immediately began exposing almost everyone with whom she had ever worked as a communist pawn. She soon became a well-known speaker, traveling the country to denounce communism.

In her public testimony before the House Un-American Activities Committee and her many lectures, Dodd explained that she had turned to communism in the early 1930s to fight fascists, but she had later concluded the CPUSA was a tool of Moscow and the Teachers Union full of Soviet sympathizers. Dodd wrote a best-selling book about her life, *School of Darkness*, published in 1954 and still in print.

At some time when she was working for the Teachers Union, Dodd and my father probably met. The union offices were at 114 East Sixteenth Street, and my father went there often to deliver his articles on Gompers High School for the union's newsletter, *Teachers News*. 114 East Sixteenth Street was also the address of the Committee for Defense of Public Education, the eloquent voice of outrage at the Rapp-Coudert Committee in the years before World War II, and the Committee for Defense of Public Education was essentially Bella Dodd. Dodd had covered the Timothy Murphy affair in scorching detail, not only in the illustrated pamphlet *New York Schools Are Invaded* but also in numerous other press releases, and it is likely she interviewed my father among other teachers at Gompers.

When Dodd embraced Catholicism and its anti-communist crusade, Moskoff turned to her to ratchet up his pursuit of members of the Teachers Union. In the early 1940s, Dodd had burned the union's membership lists so teachers could not be subpoenaed by the Rapp-Coudert Committee. Now she was willing to give Moskoff the full benefit of her memory. Still, she was an ambivalent witness. When she agreed to meet with Moskoff, she stipulated that she never be asked in public to repeat whatever information she supplied. Even when Moskoff accepted her terms, she repeatedly failed to appear for appointments.

On May 13, 1953, sixteen days after my father's interview, Dodd finally showed up at Moskoff's office, some six hours late for their most recently scheduled meeting. Instead of relying on her memory, Moskoff gave her a typed list of thirty-nine names for her to verify as present or former communists. It was a method he often used with cooperating teachers, providing names of suspects as though their guilt were already known. No betrayals were involved, Moskoff implied, since he already had these names.

That afternoon, Dodd checked off several names she thought had been Communist Party members. The last person on Moskoff's list was Saul Schur, whose name was on none of the other lists Dodd had supplied or been offered at different times. But it apparently sounded familiar. Almost done for the day, Dodd put a check by my father's name and left the office. Pleased with her cooperation, Moskoff assigned Dodd the code name "Falcon."

The next day, May 14, a teacher who had previously been called in for questioning returned to Moskoff's office, now ready to name names. Moskoff gave this teacher the code name "Parachute." Parachute named several teachers at different schools as past or present communists. He had left Gompers before my father arrived and could not remember having attended meetings together, but he recognized the name because he lived in Peter Cooper Village and often saw my father featured in *Town & Village* in connection with the PTA. After further questioning and prodding from Moskoff, Parachute decided he must have met my father at meetings of "the communist group" at Gompers, even though a few minutes earlier he had denied they worked there at the same time.

These were the shreds of Moskoff's "proof" that my father was a communist subversive. An anonymous claim from 1940, lurking in the Murphy investigation files, that called Saul a communist because he was on the editorial board of the Gompers newspaper and advisor to the Social Club. A 1941 letter Saul had written to the New York State governor decrying the treatment of City College teacher Morris Schappes, preserved in the files of the Rapp-Coudert Committee and shared with the Board of Education. A check mark from Bella Dodd, who may have met Saul in the years before World War II. A recovered memory, also from more than a decade before, from a teacher eager to please Moskoff and ready to follow his prompt. Now another distant memory from another anxious teacher, produced only after prodding and very possibly bogus, that directly contradicted a statement earlier in the same conversation. And, finally, Saul's uncooperative combativeness at his own interview.

It was more than enough.

CHAPTER 19

The House I Live In

During the years of loyalty oaths and investigations both national and local, many liberals, including my father, were suspected of being "un-American." What did that even mean?

To start, there had to be a clear definition of Americanism, which of course did not and cannot exist. The United States is only one of several nations occupying the landmass called the Americas. Even those states that form the United States, joined as they are under a single federal government, are fractiously different in their laws, their populations, and their histories. The residents of any given state hardly form a monolith as far as their backgrounds, experiences, and beliefs are concerned. As for what constitutes loyalty, patriotism, or the even more nebulous "Americanism," those are qualities most often invoked in the negative, as accusations of disloyalty, unpatriotic activities, or, particularly in the 1950s, un-Americanism. Such accusations are always made by people who feel they understand their country so well their terms need not be defined. Far too often, the attacks are directed at people who don't quite fit the accusers' conception of what an ideal American should look, sound, or think like, because a true American can only be a mirror image of themselves.

To someone like my father, schooled in patriotism and civic responsibility, being accused of "un-American" or "disloyal" behavior cut deep into his sense of self. Today, native-born American citizens of Asian, South Asian, or African descent know and fear the hostility behind the frequent question, "Where are you from?" Saul was an

Our all-American living room, inspired by the American Wing of the Metropolitan Museum of Art. Credit: Collection of the author.

American, born in Brooklyn, and he had never been out of the country. Furthermore, he had become a teacher at a time when getting certified involved daunting tests of cultural literacy. He had mastered a curriculum that celebrated the Protestant writers of New England, writers alien to his own experience. He had passed Board of Education qualifying exams that tested not only his academic subject knowledge but also his pronunciation, his dress, and his deportment— all hurdles designed to eliminate any deviation from the rather narrow norms of the examiners. And still, it seemed, he was suspected of foreign loyalties by the very educational system that had shaped him.

For both my parents, the accusation of un-American behavior was more than an insult. It attacked their conviction, so deep that it was automatic and unconscious, that they had as much a right as anyone to the principles and privileges of what was, after all, their native land. They had no nostalgic attachment to their ancestor's European origins. When asked, they could never say with any precision where their own parents had been born, and they never seemed particularly interested in finding out. Instead, they assumed they were the heirs to a national heritage that preceded the arrival of their own families.

As I went through my mother's office after her death, my father's file of mysterious character references was not the only unexpected find. I also discovered an oversized beige cardboard art portfolio, 20 by 26 inches, that had been gathering dust behind a file cabinet for a very long time. Inside, there was a drawing I had never seen before but recognized at once: a pencil sketch of our living room in Stuyvesant Town, done by an artist of obvious skill. Even if I hadn't remembered the furniture, which I certainly did, the drawing was inscribed on the bottom, "Living Room of Mr. and Mrs. Saul Schur."

What was this? Had my parents commissioned a portrait of their completely ordinary living room, with its hodgepodge of colonial-style artifacts that followed us to the suburbs a few years later and remained in use for the next thirty years? That was hard to imagine and also hard to reconcile with the fact that this drawing had never, to my knowledge, been displayed. The work was undated, but the artist's signature was clear: Edward Caswell.

I had some difficulty identifying the sources of this drawing, but over time I found some shreds of relevant information in auction catalogs, museum inventories, and a 2013 profile in *The Villager* by Suzan Mazur. Edward Caswell turned out to have had a long career as an illustrator in New York City. He had traveled in Europe in the 1920s, where he developed a knack for quaint street scenes. After he returned to New York in 1930, he applied his talents to recording the vanishing oddities of Greenwich Village. In the early 1950s, when he was almost seventy, Caswell became the resident artist for *Town & Village*, the newspaper I had pored over for information on the fight for new schools.

To find out more, I returned to New Rochelle and the bound volumes of *Town & Village* housed in the offices of Hagedorn Communications. I had already seen many examples of Caswell's work, but I hadn't been paying attention. I now realized that the front page of every issue of *Town & Village* in the early 1950s featured a large Caswell drawing, usually either a vanishing corner of old Greenwich Village or a bustling construction site along the East River, where the United

Nations international headquarters was only one of the new buildings changing the local skyline. Inside the paper, Caswell portrayed a different Stuyvesant Town or Peter Cooper Village living room every week, showing how some of the thousands of tenants living in almost identical apartments had made the space their own. Now the pencil drawing I had found in that dusty portfolio made sense. After his weekly sketch was printed in the paper, Caswell evidently gave the drawing to the family whose home was featured.

Caswell's column was called The House I Live In. This was also the name of a popular song and an award-winning short film starring Frank Sinatra, made at the end of World War II to combat anti-Semitism and promote racial tolerance. The song had been written in 1942 with music by Earl Robinson, who was blacklisted in the 1950s, and lyrics by Abel Meeropol, who with his wife Anne later adopted Julius and Ethel Rosenberg's sons after their parents were executed as communist spies. There was considerable irony in taking this title for a weekly series depicting the living rooms of a housing development that not only refused to rent to African Americans but also unofficially separated Protestants, Catholics, and Jews. Still, the publisher of *Town & Village* liked the title, and that is what he used.

After considerable searching, I found my own family living room in the paper of May 14, 1953. Like kindergartners selected to be Star of the Week, we were having our moment of glory. The text that accompanied Caswell's drawing was both accurate and highly nonsensical. My mother obviously dictated it, if she didn't in fact write it herself (late at night, on the blue typing paper she favored, working at the trusty portable typewriter that saw her through many deadlines). There were descriptions of my toy stove, my brother's collection of maps and comic books, and the many space-saving ideas that made our apartment both efficient and homey. We were a child-centered family, with a teacher father and a devoted wife and mother who, oh yes, happened to have a job.

I couldn't tell if it was pure coincidence that the feature appeared just two weeks after my father's visit to Saul Moskoff's office, or if the whole article was a deliberate effort to confirm his credentials as an upstanding citizen. My mother was entirely capable of engineering such a PR stunt, though I have no way of knowing if she did. Certainly, she seemed to feel it was important to defend her own credentials as a homemaker in an era that frowned on professional women.

Whatever the motives, the drawing revealed something very important: my parents' fervent desire to be surrounded by Americana and their wholehearted embrace of a culture very distant from the heritage of their immigrant parents. Not for us the inherited samovars from the Old Country or the proudly avant-garde paintings of other living rooms I had seen while searching through the pages of *Town & Village*. The pencil portrait of our living room confirmed that we lived in a shrine to all-American patriotic taste.

It was also an unconscious tribute to the power of the Metropolitan Museum of Art, a place my parents adored. One of the memorable expressions of my father's deep alienation from his older brother was his outrage that my cousin, Leonard's daughter, had never been to the Metropolitan Museum until my father took her there. To him, the Met, like school, was a necessary cultural experience. And, like school, it was educational. Now I wondered what he had learned.

The Metropolitan Museum opened its American Wing on November 10, 1924, little more than a year after my father posed for his graduation picture beneath the giant American flag. Like the public school curriculum of the 1920s, designed to educate the children of immigrants with a heavy diet of patriotic history and literature, the newly displayed arts of Colonial and Federalist America reflected both the ideals and the goals of the donors and curators.

R.T.H. Halsey, chair of the museum's Committee on American Decorative Arts, spoke at length at the opening about the crucial role the American Wing would play for immigrants and ethnic minorities, one of several speeches published by the museum as *Addresses on the Occasion of the Opening of the American Wing*. Exposing the masses to the culture of the founding fathers was an urgent business, Halsey felt. "Old New York has gone," he lamented at the opening of his address. "Many of our people are not cognizant of our traditions and the principles for which our fathers struggled and died. The tremendous changes in the character of our nation and the influx of foreign ideas utterly at variance with those held by the men who gave us the Republic threaten, and unless checked may shake, the foundations of our Republic."

These ignorant newcomers could now immerse themselves in a different, better culture, Halsey continued, one with traditions "invaluable in the Americanization of many of our people to whom much of our history has been hidden in a fog of unenlightenment."

If you looked at the drawing of our living room, you could see the triumph of that Americanization. My parents had often visited the museum when they were newly married, back in the days when admission was free most days of the week. In 1941, the same year Saul entered the secret files of the New York City Police Department Special Unit, my parents hired a carpenter to build a large pine wall of shelves and cupboards modeled on my father's sketches of a colonial-era fireplace wall they loved in the American Wing. The fireplace in our wall was nonfunctional, but the wood was stained a shade called Ipswich Pine, named after the town founded in 1634 by a son of the governor of the original Massachusetts Bay Colony. You could not get much more connected to early America than that.

My mother loved to tell the story of this fireplace wall, inspired by the Metropolitan Museum's American Wing, and it was retold in "The House I Live In" feature. The wall had already graced two other apartments before settling in Stuyvesant Town and becoming the centerpiece of Caswell's drawing. The living room also held a rocking chair in a Federalist Period style introduced in 1808 and a sofa that looked like a Revolutionary Era wing chair stretched to seat four people. A painted tole tray like ones that might have graced colonial tea tables sat on the fireplace mantle, along with copper beakers. On the coffee table was a pewter porringer shaped like the silver ones Paul Revere had made. Hidden in a drawer was my mother's cherished collection of antique coin silver teaspoons—thin, fragile pieces hand-hammered before the widespread introduction of machine-made silverware in the 1840s. There was other furniture, too—an end table from Macy's, a footstool from I know not where, lamps more functional than historical, a set of hideous drapes—but it was the early American touches that set the tone.

My parents' nationalist aesthetic extended beyond their furniture choices. On weekends when we were piled into the car for a family outing, the destination was often a Colonial-era house museum like the Morris-Jumel Mansion in Upper Manhattan's Washington Heights or the Bartow-Pell Mansion, near where the Bronx touches Westchester County. Longer trips would take us to Sturbridge Village in Massachusetts, a recreation of an early New England town, where we happily ate Indian pudding and had a family photo taken while imprisoned in the stocks. Did my parents feel they were being Americanized, or did they consider their taste for all things early American a triumph over those who dismissed them, their parents, their neighbors, and their schoolmates as unenlightened barbarians? I suspect they didn't think in those terms at all. They were Americans, born and bred, as entitled to cornhusk dolls and ladderback chairs as they were to chewing gum or subway rides—or so they thought.

Just below the portrait of our family living room in *Town & Village* was a large advertisement for the Home Mortgage Clinic of First Federal Savings Bank. "Planning to Buy or Build Your Dream House?" the advertisers asked. A third baby was on the way and my parents were eager to buy a house, or at least my mother was. Not the one-story house the bank was advertising, either. For the next two years, I heard her tell friends, relatives, realtors, really anyone who would listen, that she wanted a center-entry colonial house. But this was not a time to be looking at real estate.

Two days after our living room appeared in *Town & Village*, one day after Bella Dodd checked his name on Moskoff's list and a full month before the end of the academic year, my father submitted his formal resignation. It was a bitter decision. Seeing how soon his resignation followed Moskoff's dogged prodding of possible informants, I suppose my father must have gotten word that the Board of Education was intent on pursuing a formal hearing on his "insubordination" and "conduct unbecoming a teacher." His careful preparation for the Moskoff interview had been fruitless. His citing of board decisions in the Murphy case had been brushed aside. His long years of devotion to teaching and his many official commendations had been ignored. Whatever lingered of the shining vision of American justice Saul had learned as a child had turned out to be deeply tarnished. If he did not resign, he and his family would be dragged into the spotlight before a public tribunal—after which he would undoubtedly be fired.

His letter of resignation was terse. Addressed to Dr. William Jansen, Superintendent of Schools, and dated May 19, it read:

Dear Sir:
After sixteen years as an appointed teacher of English in the New York City high school division, it is with deep regret that I submit to you my resignation from this post effective Monday, May 25, 1953.

On May 20, even before the resignation had taken effect, Jansen ordered "the usual letter" be placed in my father's file, citing evidence "tending to indicate" that he had been "a member of or affiliated with" the Communist Party while a teacher. The purpose of this form letter was to block any later attempt at reinstatement.

My father could and did find another job, but not the job he wanted, as a teacher in the city schools. Underpaid, ill used, and largely unappreciated, he had been doing what he loved. As for any students he might have had at the High School for Aviation Arts, so suddenly abandoned just before final exams, they were left to stumble forward as best they could.

CHAPTER 20

What Made Them So Afraid?

As I went ever deeper into my own investigation of the New York City Board of Education's anti-communist measures and into the broader history of blacklists and purges across the country in the 1950s, I came to a much better understanding of the resigned detachment that was a mark of my father's personality in his later years. As much as I learned, though, I still couldn't answer a simple question: What made the investigators so afraid?

Like their fellow inquisitors, past and present, William Jansen and Saul Moskoff had little concrete evidence to justify their purges. Both men frequently declared that a teacher with any exposure of any kind to communist or socialist thought would be working—inevitably, inexorably—to undermine the government of the United States. Both men were stubbornly resistant to the alternate possibility, that they themselves were undermining the constitutional rights that underpin our democratic society.

But where did they get those beliefs? The teachers and staff who were hounded out of their jobs in New York City and other districts around the country were not privy to any government secrets or information useful to enemy states. They worked at overcrowded, underfunded public schools where they were holding their own against chaos, not leading a revolution. But that did nothing to stop the new legion of anti-communist crusaders from scouring the schools.

Trying to understand the mindset of the Board of Education's investigators, I took a deep and sobering plunge into hyperconservative literature of the Cold War era, the print precursors of today's Fox News

and myriad online sites catering to conspiracy theorists and provoca-
teurs. To be an active, engaged conservative in the 1950s was to embrace
a daily barrage of baseless accusations that created, affirmed, and solidified extremist ideologies. The details were many, varied, and frequently absurd, but the message was always that America was in grave
danger from subversive forces, a conviction reinforced by the inflam-
matory publications that the target audience read, discussed, and
shared among each other.

Sometimes readers also saved these messages, leaving them like buried land mines to wait for some unknown future audience. Almost by
accident, I was introduced to a vast archive of mid-century conservative literature amassed in Pasadena, California, a hotbed of conservative activism in the 1950s and 1960s. The collector, Marie Koenig, acted
locally but collected material that was national in scope. And much of
it was about the perils of "socialist" education, with a surprising focus
on far-away New York.

By this time, I thought I knew a lot about Cold War paranoia. Now,
as I turned the pages of broadsides, pamphlets, neighborhood newsletters, action memos, and fundraising appeals, I realized I hadn't com-
prehended its breadth or fully tasted its venom. I was pummeled by
screeds warning of the looming apocalypse posed by everything from
the United Nations to parent-teacher conferences. I read improbable
rants about secret cells of Soviet-controlled subversives trained to introduce fluoride to municipal water supplies, along with numerous false
claims that fluoride, a naturally occurring mineral, was a narcotic and
an agent of mind control. Fluoridation, like the twenty-first-century
battles over vaccination, had become a proxy for government control
of mind and body.

Another danger that loomed large in the minds of 1950s conservatives was the mimeograph machine, the precursor of the photocopier.
In the fearful years of communist investigations, knowing how to use
a mimeograph machine was considered a possible sign of communist
indoctrination. Herbert Philbrick recounted in *I Led 3 Lives* how he
was allowed to use the mimeograph machine at his local Communist
Party headquarters, proof of how trusted he had become. Another
former Communist Party member, eager to renounce his sins, said he

had been trained to disassemble and reassemble a mimeograph machine in the dark, like a soldier drilled in taking apart his rifle and putting it back together. I laughed out loud when I read that, dismissing it as a paranoid fever dream. But the mimeograph machine, like all methods of disseminating information, could indeed be a weapon. I thought back to all those blue stencils on my father's bedroom desk. As far as I can tell, he was just typing up the PTA newsletter.

Among the anti-communist pamphlets and weekly letters to subscribers, I also saw a dispiriting number of viciously anti-Semitic cartoons. Other graphics identified the crucifix and other specifically Christian emblems as essential pillars of liberty, burying the ideals of secular society under a slag pile of religious and racial intolerance.

Within this raging storm of anxiety, within which just about anything could be perceived as a source of personal and national peril, many warnings were about teachers, and especially about teachers in New York City. Over and over—in books, pamphlets, newsletters, broadsides, and action memos, many printed with the alarmingly varied typefaces usually reserved for bomb threats and ransom notes—I found the same urgent messages. Communism was the greatest threat to America's future. Progressive teachers were agents of communism, intent on corrupting children to their views. And New York City teachers—notoriously liberal, cosmopolitan, and Jewish—were expressly devoted to teaching the overthrow of the United States "by force or violence." Laws against overthrowing the government "by force or violence" had been introduced as early as 1940. By the 1950s, the phrase seemed to be everywhere, as essential as the words "under God" inserted in the Pledge of Allegiance in 1953.

The anti-communist literature I read was churned out by a small but prolific cadre of publishers who generally ignored traditional bookstores or reviewers to concentrate their marketing on the already converted. Liberty Bell Press, the Constitution and Free Enterprise Foundation, Henry Regnery, Caxton Printers, and Devin-Adair, Inc. all advertised heavily in conservative media and gave readers deep discounts for quantity orders, urging "concerned citizens" to buy in bulk and distribute their literature to sympathetic audiences. Like highly partisan online sites today, posting and reposting their alarmist screeds, far-right publishers of the 1950s created a closed echo chamber of constant agitation and aggression.

Pamphlets, magazines, and newsletters were equally extreme—both in their attacks on teachers and in their fervor to wrap themselves in the mystic aura of "Americanism." The American Legion, the national organization of U.S. military veterans formed immediately after World War I, had taken a strong anti-communist turn by the 1940s, including compiling secret lists of supposed subversives for FBI director J. Edgar Hoover and trying to introduce its own ideologically conservative textbooks to public schools. An article in *American Legion Magazine* from June 1952, "Your Child Is Their Target," detailed "the amazing story of how our public educational system has been, in many instances, diverted from its traditional purpose of imparting sound basic education to the ideological purpose of creating a new society based on the economic, social and political doctrines of collectivism or socialism."

Other organizations with a national audience also warned about the rising threat to what they called "traditional values" in the schools. The American Education Association's slogan was "Keep Our American Schools American," which apparently meant something very specific to the association's members. The American Parents Committee on Education stated that its mission was "to expose and root out un-American activities in our educational system." The Church League of America trampled the traditional separation of church and state while sounding the alarm in pamphlets like *Can We Preserve Our "American System" in the Postwar World?*

Facts in Education, a weekly newsletter published by a Pasadena group called Pro-America, repeatedly branded contemporary education as "casual," by which they meant lacking intellectual content or rigor. *Facts in Education* also warned against teaching "human relations," a phrase the group used as a dog whistle for racial integration. Pro-America's members considered racial equality, at home or in school, to be the opening wedge for a communist takeover. *Facts in Education* also denounced a 1950 summer conference organized by Willard Goslin, the embattled superintendent of the Pasadena school system, not only because Goslin supported the un-American cause of racial integration but also because he had invited a speaker from New York City, well known as the epicenter of evil. Among his other sins, Goslin had distributed a pamphlet that *Facts in Education* noted was "put out by B'nai B'rith's 'Anti-Defamation League.'" This yet again reflected and perpetuated the conservative view that all Jews were communists.

Goslin, the offending organizer of the conference, was a nationally recognized educator and president of the well-respected American Association of School Administrators. In 1947, when he was superintendent of schools in Minneapolis, Goslin had been a leading candidate for the job of New York City superintendent of schools that eventually went to William Jansen. By 1950, his belief in "un-American" ideas like integration was about to cost him his current position in Pasadena.

Whether in a local newsletter like *Facts in Education* or a glossy national publication like the *American Legion Magazine*, accusations routinely leaped from the individual classroom to national villains to the end of civilization as we know it. Along with communists and leftist teachers, two recurrent enemies were Eleanor Roosevelt and the United Nations. Mrs. Roosevelt was an immensely popular national figure, both as First Lady and after her husband's death in 1945 as the country's first delegate to the United Nations, where she chaired the UN Commission on Human Rights. To ultraconservatives, however, she was a dupe, a spy, and very probably an outright communist agent. As for the United Nations, it was considered a subversive organization that threatened to nullify the U.S. Constitution. Nobody ever explained how this was going to happen, but everyone knew (Knew! *Knew!*) it was true. Therefore, the UN had to be kicked out of the country and all references to the sinister organization had to be purged from textbooks.

I grew up very near the United Nations headquarters on the Manhattan side of the East River, and I had a very different impression of the place. The rising complex of striking modern buildings was a glamorous neighbor less than two miles from our Stuyvesant Town apartment, and my father would always point it out on car rides. I could admire the tall glass tower of the Secretariat Building and the low, curving facade of the General Assembly Building. One hot summer day when I was five or six, I even tried to walk there myself, following the pedestrian path along the East River.

When the UN was completed and the public was allowed inside, we made a family visit. The Security Council chamber was impressive, but to me it was overshadowed by the fascination of the Foucault pendulum, a dangling weight that marked the earth's rotation by tracing curved lines in a circular sand pit visible below the viewers' railing. In the gift shop, I could buy tiny "worry dolls" from Peru and even tinier red seeds from India that had been hollowed out to hold a troop of minuscule ivory elephants. As far as I could tell, one of the messages of the UN headquarters was that the rest of the world existed to provide trinkets for American children.

In the 1950s, it would never have occurred to me that the United Nations was an existential threat to democracy. By the time I finished kindergarten, I knew enough about atom bombs to long for world peace. When told to make a wish—over a birthday candle, a wishbone, a first star—I always wished someone would do away with the bombs that my classmates said could kill us in a burning flash. The United Nations was all about world peace, so I was for it. As for Eleanor Roosevelt, the fact that my father offered her as a character witness in his interview with Moskoff suggests that he shared my ignorance of how the former First Lady was demonized by the hyperconservative press.

According to the publications I was now reading, my father and I (and too many others) were blind to the danger right before us. The May 1951 bulletin of *News and Views*, for example, warned readers of the "Menace of the 'Left-Coalition.'" Conceding that "there are not enough avowed Communists or outright Socialists to push a national structure like ours away from its basic traditions" (rooted in Christianity and free enterprise, of course), the editors listed elements of the "secret manipulative alliance" that was propelling the nation dangerously "*Leftward!*" The list started with communists and socialists, followed immediately by New Dealers and internationalists ("those who are for 'America last,'—those who continually indulge in national self-abasement . . . those who have a militant and abnormal obsession on 'brotherhood'"). After that came labor union supporters, racial-consciousness groups, supporters of federal spending programs, private foundations that gave money to liberal causes, "columnists and commentators who slant their presentations purposely to collaborate with the Left-wing movement," and even socialites and social climbers who followed voguish ideas, presumably including world peace. In the end, the list of suspects appeared to include everyone who was not an active reader of *News and Views*.

As I read on, I was told that creeping internationalism wasn't the only threat that had to be purged from schools. An even greater danger, it seemed, was collectivism, a term that right-wing fearmongers applied to just about anything that might interfere with the competitive spirit they hailed as the backbone of American ideals.

Here's an example. Guardians of American Education described itself in 1950 as "an independent organization devoted to preserving the principles of the Declaration of Independence and the Constitution of the United States in our schools and colleges." Its main publication was a weekly newsletter, available by paid subscription, that hardly varied in content but always managed to be urgent and terrifying about the communist menace lurking in America's public schools. One of its most effective products, though, was a simple wall chart.

This handy poster, some 24 by 36 inches, compared "up-to-date traditional values" to the "training for collectivism" of public schools infiltrated by subversive agents of dangerous ideas. It attacked what it called the collectivism of after-school activities, the relativism of teacher conferences, the communist recommendations of the American Library Association (which praised books about sharing, among other suspect concepts), and the socialist theories of progressive educator John Dewey, whose death in 1952 at age ninety-two would do nothing to spare him from attack.

According to the Guardians of American Education chart, properly educated students should receive at least six report cards a year, with class ranks calculated to the third decimal, "to enable child and parent to know what proportion of the work expected of the child he has mastered." By contrast, the chart warned, "progress reports" without numerical grades would lead to "the elimination of individualism and the competitive spirit as a means of eliminating the free enterprise feature of American society." "Up-to-date traditional" music and art classes should be limited to one hour a week, to supplement instruction that should properly be given at home, while "training for collectivism" music programs encouraged socialist tendencies through group participation and the loaning of musical instruments without charge.

At this point, I gave up searching for logic in the literature of provocation. There are many reasons to oppose communism, but the subversive danger of school orchestras is not among them. I would have to look elsewhere for explanations.

CHAPTER 21

The Fear Profiteers

In education and in politics, and particularly in the politics of education, it is always useful to follow the money. The hunt for un-American activities provided a good living for many of the fearmongers who made a career out of searching for subversives, an income that rose in inverse proportion to the accuracy of their reports. The broadsides I was reading were little known outside of their own conservative circles. But in that space there was a lot of money to be made.

As happens today, calculating opportunists profited financially by stirring hatred and fear, creating a rabid audience that demanded ever more strident, more frequent, more lurid—and more lucrative—attacks. In the 2020s, conspiracy theorists use their online platforms to sell hats, T-shirts, quack diets, and other high-profit trash. In the 1950s, the product was simpler. They were selling fear itself, packaged and repackaged in pamphlets, books, posters, and speaking engagements.

Some of the individuals who made money fighting communism were very well known. Herbert Philbrick, for example, became an instant national celebrity after his explosive testimony in the 1949 anti-communist trial in Manhattan. His memoir, *I Led 3 Lives*, was published in 1952 to great success. In January 1953, Philbrick's lawyer reported that he had been offered two million dollars (equivalent to over $23 million today) for the television rights to what became the very popular weekly program by the same name. At the time, Philbrick was also in separate talks with Hollywood for a film version. Thus, Philbrick profited first as a paid informant for the FBI and then much more amply by selling the print, television, and film versions of his story. I doubt Philbrick became a double agent for the money, but he didn't scorn the rewards or fail to hire a good agent. Actor Richard Carlson, who played Philbrick on television, also profited from the general paranoia of the time. While he was appearing weekly on television in *I Led 3 Lives*, he also starred in *The Creature from the Black Lagoon* and *It Came from Outer Space*, two films that dealt with the terror of alien takeovers in more metaphorical ways.

People who didn't have Philbrick's celebrity found other ways to make money by searching for subversives. The FBI used paid informers, several of whom were coached to implicate innocent people and all of whom were generously compensated for their services. Contemporary reports suggest many informants were paid at least ten thousand dollars a year by the FBI—about twice the annual salary of the average New York City high school teacher. If they testified in court as "expert consultants," they might be paid another nine or ten thousand dollars a year. Matt Cvetic, a professional informer in Pittsburgh who was on the FBI payroll, also collected $12,500 for the movie rights to his story and another $6,500 for a series of magazine articles.

Louis Budenz was a former communist and labor union activist who, like Bella Dodd, was "returned" to the Roman Catholic Church by the popular television priest Fulton Sheen and then profited from his new career as an anti-communist informer. From 1945 to 1957, Budenz was paid at least $60,000 for various magazine articles, books, and lectures, in addition to witness fees and direct payments of over $70,000 from the FBI. In over 3,000 hours of interviews for the FBI, over thirty appearances before congressional committees, and numerous appearances at trials of alleged communists, Budenz popularized the principle adopted by Saul Moskoff in the New York City school investigations that all communists were instructed to lie, and therefore anyone who denied communist affiliations was not to be believed. If that person was a witness in court, he or she could be convicted of perjury, a policy followed in the New York City school investigative trials.

The New York City Board of Education didn't have the budget of the FBI, but that didn't mean Moskoff was unwilling to pay for information. The most famous informer on the New York City payroll was an opportunistic young man named Harvey Matusow. Matusow joined the Communist Party in 1947, when he was twenty, and then worked for three years with youth groups and as a clerk in the Communist Party bookstore in Manhattan. After that, he turned to better-paid employment as a professional informer.

Starting with his collaboration with the FBI in 1950, Matusow profited repeatedly from his former communist connections by working for the House Un-American Activities Committee; the Senate Internal Security Subcommittee; and *Counterattack*, the FBI-supported publication best known for *Red Channels*, its list of suspect artists and performers that became the handbook of radio, television, and Hollywood blacklists. Matusow's activities ranged from recording license plates of cars arriving at a "liberal" ranch in New Mexico to testifying against the editors of *People's Song*, an early folk music magazine that featured labor union songs. His testimony contributed to the black-listing of Pete Seeger, Alan Lomax, Lee Hays, and other stalwarts of the folk music revival.

In February 1952, while my father was leading parent groups to Board of Estimate meetings to beg for new classrooms, Moskoff hired Matusow to work as an informer for the New York City Board of Education. The salary was twenty-five dollars a day—excellent pay at the time. Matusow did not last long, losing his job when he tried to involve Moskoff's assistant in a kickback scheme. But that didn't discredit the information he had provided. Instead, Moskoff invented a false name for himself, Nat Moss, and used it to make telephone calls to check details Matusow had only vaguely remembered. Moskoff was proud of his deception (another sign of his theatrical bent) and of his calls. As he recorded in his notes, the calls were simply to confirm names. Matusow's contributions as an informer before he was fired was accepted without question.

Like Philbrick, Budenz, and Dodd, Matusow tried to capitalize further by writing a tell-all book. *False Witness* was published in 1955. Sadly for Matusow, his royalties were smaller than Philbrick's and his troubles greater. In *False Witness*, Matusow claimed that he had lied under oath and had been coached to do so by Senator Joseph McCarthy's lawyer, Roy Cohn. In a suitably farcical twist, Matusow was then tried for perjury and sentenced to five years in prison for lying under oath when he testified that he previously had lied under oath—a conviction that served mainly to protect those he had both duped and exposed. Cohn was unscathed by the accusation of witness tampering.

Matusow went on to multiple marriages and a head-spinning string of careers as art cataloger, music promoter, founder of the Society for the Abolition of Data Processing Machines, and clown for a traveling children's theater before, eventually, converting to Mormonism. He never matched the financial success he enjoyed as a paid informer, when his information was accepted as true even amid the growing evidence of his unstable and unscrupulous character.

Informers like Philbrick, Dodd, Budenz, and Matusow were just the best known of a vast network of speakers and writers who made their living preaching against the menace of "collectivism." Conservative organizations with bland names but toxic agendas actively promoted a harrowing image of schools overrun by subversive teachers intent on brainwashing their students. They sent speakers (for a fee) to address local groups across the country and encouraged their listeners to subscribe to newsletters and buy books, pamphlets, and posters. The Church League of America, publisher of *News and Views,* with its alarming list of leftist conspirators, became a compiler and seller of anti-communist research in the 1950s, its operations directed by a former Air Force intelligence officer. The Church League continued to sell reports and charge for access to its library well into the 1980s.

New York City, the unnervingly cosmopolitan metropolis that inspired so much fear, was also a center for the anti-communist industry. For my own family, the people who profited by demonizing teachers were close at hand—a fact that would have been distressing if we had known of their existence. Guardians of American Education, publishers of that extraordinary wall chart attacking parent-teacher conferences and school orchestras, had its office at 225 Fifth Avenue in Manhattan, an easy half-hour walk from our Stuyvesant Town door. A different thirty-minute stroll could have taken us to the Committee on Education, at 112 East Thirty-Sixth Street, which published the *Educational Reviewer* to evaluate textbooks and other school material—because even conservative school boards could not be trusted to screen for possible socialist influences. America's Future, headquartered at 210 East Forty-Third Street, thirty blocks north of our apartment, hammered at what it saw as pernicious influences in the schools, with a special emphasis on union membership as a sign of a subversive teacher. In books and pamphlets peppered with fevered capital letters, America's Future never tired of warning against the "Socialist Menace to America's Way of Life."

The American Education Association, an organization of conservative New York City teachers formed by Milo Francis McDonald, principal of Bushwick High School in Brooklyn, had its offices at 545 Fifth Avenue, a little over two miles from our apartment. In language that was prevalent in many fear-mongering speeches at the time and seems to be making a comeback today, McDonald campaigned constantly against the evils of "progressive" education. As he wrote in his 1951 book, *Progressive Poison in Public Education*, "All 'progressive' education is dangerous. It threatens our American way of life to which our American youth should be passionately devoted. It is a way of life we wish them to be zealous to preserve, a way of life that spells opportunity to preserve the gifts to humanity of Christianity upon which all true democracy is built." McDonald makes clear what is implied by many others—the campaign against progressive ideas was a crusade to enforce Christianity and eliminate godless radicals, a category that includes even the most observant Jews.

A particularly egregious fear-for-profit operation was something called the National Council for American Education, located in Lower Manhattan and, again, an easy walk from our front door. Allen Zoll, founder and self-elected president of the National Council for American Education, was a hate-monger for hire who traveled around the country encouraging school districts to oust progressive teachers and principals. Zoll charged significant fees for his speeches and for newsletters like *Facts in Education* and *Educational Guardian*, among other titles. He was also the author of pamphlets with provocative titles like *They WANT Your Child*, *Progressive Education Increases Delinquency*, and *REDucators at Harvard*, all of which were for sale at prices that compared with those of national magazines. Membership in the National Council for American Education cost from $5 for an associate member to $1,000, the price of the "Benefactor" level.

Zoll was also a professional hater of Jews, a career that preceded but overlapped with his for-profit crusade against liberal education and progressive educators. In July 1939, after the National Association of Broadcasters refused to air Father Coughlin's racist and anti-Semitic programs, Zoll had been charged with extortion for demanding payment from a radio station owner to call off his group's pickets demanding Coughlin's return. Coughlin, of course, was one of the chief promoters of the belief that teachers, and especially New York City teachers, were active agents of communist insurrection.

The same year that Zoll was trying to extort money from radio station owners, my father and his fellow teachers were pressing their case against Timothy Murphy for racist, anti-Semitic, and pro-fascist acts at Gompers High School. Zoll was an associate of George Timone, who helped organize the fascist rally at Madison Square Garden. This was the same Timone who joined the New York City Board of Education in 1950 and authored the notorious Timone Resolution, stripping teachers of their civil rights.

Well into the 1950s, while selling his services as a guardian of educational standards, Zoll also worked as a fundraiser for anti-Semitic, racist political commentators like Gerald L. K. Smith, Elizabeth Dilling, and Josef Washington Hall, who for some reason preferred to be known as Upton Close. One of Close's favorite themes was the communist threat to American education. On November 15, 1946, just as the post–World War II Red Scare was beginning, the *Brooklyn Daily Eagle* reported that Close was urging listeners to "keep pushing until they eradicate the great menace of Communism, which had been permitted to operate too long—until it almost dominated our school system."

By 1951, Close's programs had become so virulent that his organization, Broadcast, Inc., lost its tax-exempt status as an educational institution. By then, Close had reportedly paid Zoll a $30,000 commission for his fundraising efforts, proving once again that being a professional hater of liberal teachers was a route to profit as well as power. And meanwhile, credulous readers and listeners became ever more convinced that individual teachers were actively working to brainwash children as a way of destroying the country.

Whether they were true believers or cynical profiteers, the people behind the attacks on liberal teachers had a powerful and harmful influence. Rabidly prejudiced broadcasters like Close, pamphlet factories like Guardians of American Education, and agile alarmists like

Zoll succeeded in terrifying audiences from the PTAs of suburban California to the Board of Education of New York City, the largest school system in the country. A professed "middle-of-the-roader" like Superintendent Jansen and a supporter of the Democratic Party like Moskoff no longer saw, or cared, how far they swerved into extremism. This was one of the tragedies of the 1950s, a hypervigilant moment when authoritarianism posed as prudence and clear violations of civil liberties were recast as necessary responses to vague and often fabricated threats.

CHAPTER 22

Outcast and Wanderer

When my father left teaching, he was a forty-two-year-old man with two children, a third on the way, and no idea what he was going to do for a living. From the age of five, he had spent his entire life, including his army service, in one sort of classroom or another. Now he had to find a way to exist outside of school.

He had already tried to change careers, hoping to enter the only business that stirred his passion as much as teaching English. He wanted to break into Hollywood. In the summer of 1951, when the Board of Education started to investigate some of his fellow teachers, he wrote to movie producer Cecil B. DeMille, proposing a movie version of *The Odyssey* using the approach he had found so successful in teaching Homer's epic to the students at Gompers Vocational High School.

Like most of Saul's favorite stories, *The Odyssey* is about a wanderer beset by dangers who succeeds at last through luck, guile, and strength of character. If he could get car-crazy kids interested in an ancient poem about a married soldier who takes ten years to get home from the Trojan War, he reasoned, Hollywood should be able to take it to the masses. It was only six years since the end of World War II, and my father imagined that audiences could identify with the story of the weary veteran who finds it difficult to return to his former life.

Saul's appeal to DeMille was doomed in several ways. It was wildly ambitious, if not outright delusional, to think that the most successful director in Hollywood, one of the founders of the film industry, would hire an unknown high school English teacher as his consulting muse. Nor was Hollywood any sort of refuge from blacklists; the 1947 refusals to testify at congressional hearings that led to jail sentences for the so-called Hollywood Ten was extremely well publicized. DeMille was also much in the news, not only as a producer but also as a conservative Republican who actively supported anti-communist investigations, loyalty oaths, and other repressive measures.

The attempt to become a Hollywood advisor seems both desperate and ludicrous. Did my father somehow think he and DeMille would get along, just as he had thought he could appeal to the Parkchester Christian Association to join the defense of Morris Schappes, the fired communist teacher at City College? He had no chance to find out. The producer brushed Saul off with a very polite letter, using extremely handsome stationery that would find its place in the file of blacklist memorabilia.

Undaunted, my father next approached Laurence Olivier, the celebrated English stage actor and theater manager who had recently moved to Hollywood and resumed his career in film. Once again, this unknown teacher's offer to consult on a film version of *The Odyssey* was declined, again on elegant stationery that has scarcely faded over time. Still, it hadn't been a bad idea. Three years later, Kirk Douglas starred in *Ulysses*, which was filmed in Italy and produced by Carlo Ponti and Dino di Laurentis. The movie was a huge success, part of a newly popular genre of action movies featuring swords and sandals. Unfortunately, nobody invited my father to Rome to consult.

Rebuffed by Hollywood, Saul stayed in his teaching job and devoted the next two years to campaigning for relief from overcrowded schools. That was an epic battle he won, but by the spring of 1953 he was out of the classroom and no longer active in the PTA. Cast adrift from the schools that had always been his anchor, he was terrified. Eventually, like most of the blacklisted teachers, he managed to forge a new life. It was not the life he had imagined, and it was not a choice he willingly made, but he would survive. My parents stayed married, although I'm sure there were strains and compromises. If the stress and disappointment left any psychological scars on me or my brothers, we were unaware of them.

Were we typical of families affected by the New York City Board of Education inquisitions? For most of the blacklisted teachers, and particularly for those who were not called by any congressional committee and did not go to court to protest their case, there are no public records of what happened after losing their jobs.

There are a few clues. The internal records of Moskoff's investigations show he was convinced his duty was to get suspect teachers out of the classroom however he could, but he was not terribly concerned with what they did after that. He let several teachers and other personnel retire early for reasons that would probably not have been honored under other circumstances. Women in their forties and fifties produced letters from doctors describing their sufferings from menopausal hot flashes, a diagnosis that allowed them to retire and receive a pension while the Board of Education avoided a trial. Male teachers brought letters citing debilitating anxiety—an entirely plausible result of the treatment they had received at the hands of their inquisitor, though it did not always work as well as "female troubles." Curiously blinkered about the impact of his inquisition, Moskoff's willingness to let some teachers retire instead of being fired is the only sign that he was concerned with his victims' fates.

Teachers who chose to resign rather than face a disciplinary hearing usually found other work, though sometimes only after significant hardship. Some former public school teachers shifted to teaching in private schools, often at lower salaries and without union protections. Some opened schools for children or adults with mental, physical, or emotional challenges—populations underserved by the public schools. Several teachers went back to school and had successful careers as psychotherapists, possibly inspired by their own recent traumas and the seeming insanity of the times. Some wrote textbooks or became copywriters. Educational films and nonprofit radio programs paid less than their more commercial counterparts, but workers there were less vulnerable to the pressure of *Red Channels* because their employers had no advertisers who could be intimidated.

One teacher found work in a Christmas card production shop before becoming a remedial reading teacher at a private school. Another became a salesman for a company selling very early versions of computers, a job that paid much better than teaching but that he hated. When he died decades later and his grown children were asked his profession, they answered in unison, "He was a teacher." One of my father's colleagues at Gompers became an insurance agent, just like the all-American hero of *Father Knows Best*, which had its television premiere in 1954. He sold insurance to my family for years.

One door, however, was closed for good. Being a teacher in a public school system, no matter how far away, was nearly impossible. In 1964, a Rutgers University sociologist named Paul D. Tillett sent questionnaires to teachers and government officials for a study he titled *The Social Costs of the Loyalty Programs*. Tillett died before his study was completed, but his papers, including these questionnaires, are now at the Seeley G. Mudd Manuscript Library at Princeton University. Respondents were eager to share their stories, although many were so scarred by the experience that they insisted their replies remain anonymous. One blacklisted teacher claimed to have sent out two thousand applications for teaching positions, only 10 percent of which even got replies. None of his letters led to a job. Another teacher, fired from every job after the FBI went to employers to reveal her past, was literally forced underground by the pressure of the blacklist. To support herself, she moved into the basement of her home and rented out the rest of the house. Former teachers also reported hate mail and threatening phone calls, as well as huge financial insecurity. Blacklisted teachers in Boston, Philadelphia, Los Angeles, and Denver suffered similar fates.

In 1954, the *Denver Post* published a series of articles by associate editor Lawrence Martin that was reprinted as a pamphlet, *Faceless Informers and Our Schools*. On his way to report on the New York City investigations, Martin described arriving at Moskoff's Brooklyn office in a taxi whose driver turned out to be a former teacher. "Abandon hope all ye who enter here," the cabbie said, referring to the inscription over the gate of hell in Dante's *Inferno*. "I was called into that building. When I came out, I'd had it. They told me I was a Communist. They asked me, and then they told me. School's out, for me."

We cannot know how long this Dante-quoting cabbie stayed behind the wheel. Most of the teachers forced out of their jobs had college degrees and had risen above their college peers in very competitive exams to be qualified as teachers. Well educated by the very school system that was now intent on getting rid of them, most managed to find other kinds of work. According to a Ford Foundation report from

1953, *Teachers for Tomorrow*, teachers earned less than engineers, accountants, or salesmen. Outstanding college graduates who became teachers earned considerably less than liberal arts graduates who went into other fields, suggesting that the ousted teachers had the potential to earn at least at much outside the public school system as they did within. That year, the Ford Foundation said, the average salary of teachers in "big city high schools" was $5,560. After sixteen years on the job, my father made less.

A few of the teachers forced out of the New York City schools had well-documented careers after they left the city schools. Samuel Wallach, one of the first teachers to be fired, went on to make widely distributed educational filmstrips and, as an administrator at Maimonides Hospital, worked successfully to mainstream developmentally disabled children into schools and residential group homes.

Irving Adler, formerly a math teacher, was possibly the most successful survivor of the New York City public school teachers purge. Adler was fired from his job as a math teacher at a Manhattan vocational school, Straubenmuller Textile High School, on the grounds that he might exert a dangerous influence over his students. In his next career, he became the best-selling author of almost one hundred books of popular science and mathematics, including elementary school workbooks that sold twenty-eight million copies. Adler's *The New Mathematics* (1958) inspired the curriculum movement known by its abbreviated name, the new math. Many people hated "the new math" as a teaching tool, but there can be no doubt that Adler had much more influence over children than he could ever have exerted if he had kept his teaching job.

My father never came close to Adler's fame or commercial success, but there was one important similarity. Eventually, he, too, found a niche that gave him far greater opportunities to mold the thinking of impressionable young people than he had ever had teaching English in a vocational high school in the Bronx. That was all in the future, though. In the spring of 1953, my father had good reason to be scared.

Anti-communist hysteria was at its height. In May, the same month my father sent his resignation to the Board of Education, the State Department issued a list of banned composers, artists, and writers. May 1953 was also when Jerome Robbins, choreographer of *The King and I*, admitted his early communist ties and named former comrades before the House Committee on Un-American Activities. The next month, almost exactly twenty years after the infamous Nazi book burning in Berlin, the State Department sent instructions to burn "subversive" books in its overseas libraries. A member of the Indiana state textbook commission denounced the story of Robin Hood as communist propaganda.

All in all, it seemed prudent to keep a low profile. Moskoff was not known to pursue teachers who had resigned, but that was no guarantee he wouldn't start. If Saul's name landed in the news as a suspected subversive, it would bring personal grief and might jeopardize my mother's job just when we were completely dependent on her income. Friends who had a house in Croton-on-Hudson knew our family was in hot water, as they later described it, and offered us a retreat while they were away.

Thirty miles north of New York City, Croton-on-Hudson was an easy train ride for my mother when she needed to be at work. Six months pregnant, she was now the only breadwinner in the family and was determined to continue as food editor at *Look* magazine. Wearing a series of elegant maternity suits tailored by her father, who had worked in the garment trade when he first came to America, she perfected a frigid stare that dared any of her magazine colleagues to mention her increasingly obvious condition.

Like everything else about this story, the country idyll could also be interpreted in an incriminating way. Croton-on-Hudson had a bohemian reputation and a radical tinge that went back to the start of the twentieth century. When artists and writers started arriving from New York City, the town became known as the Greenwich Village on the Hudson. John Reed, author of *Ten Days That Shook the World*, a firsthand celebration of the Russian Revolution, had lived there with his lover and then wife Louise Bryant (played by Warren Beatty and Diane Keaton in the 1980 film *Reds*). In the 1930s, the town became a magnet for socialist and left-wing intellectuals. Mount Airy Road, where Reed and Bryant once lived, got the nickname Red Hill, in honor of its radical associations.

Coincidentally, our borrowed house was on Mount Airy Road. Novelist Howard Fast, whose novel *Citizen Tom Paine* had been banned from New York City schools at the urging of George Timone, also passed a summer in rustic exile on Mount Airy Road, just before he spent three months in prison in 1950 for contempt of Congress. In his 1990 memoir *Being Red*, Fast described the neighborhood as "a rich mixture of communists, socialists, people who were neither but loved the beauty of the place, and even here and there an anti-communist who had long since surrendered his beliefs but would not surrender his home on Mount Airy."

Fast was imprisoned for refusing to name contributors to a fund for orphans of American volunteers killed fighting to defend Spain's left-leaning government in the Spanish Civil War. The war ended in 1939, but early opposition to authoritarian regimes—what came to be called "premature anti-Fascism"—was seen as a sign of communist sympathies, a crime without an expiration date. One of the contributors to the orphans' fund was said to have been Eleanor Roosevelt, but Fast wasn't telling.

Just as the teacher purge had brought me to Broadway to see *The King and I*, our retreat to Croton-on-Hudson took me to my first movie, at the local Starlight Drive-In movie theater. Like so many other families, my parents put me in pajamas and assumed I would sleep through the whole thing, even if my older brother stayed awake. Instead, I was completely absorbed by the show, which I watched by peering through the windshield over my father's shoulder.

The film was *Stalag 17*, a tense drama about American army officers in a German prison camp trying to identify the spy in their barracks while they also plan an escape. I knew nothing of World War II, which was over before I was born. I knew nothing of Germans, the army, or the meaning of the word "traitor." What I understood very well, though, was that these guys were jumpy with anxiety and that there was a very exciting fight in a room where they all seemed to sleep in bunk beds. I had seen bunk beds in other people's apartments, and I had seen people get into fights right on the street, sometimes on my way to school, so I imagined this as some sort of large nervous family. By then, nervous families were another thing I understood.

New York was in the middle of a heat wave when we returned to Stuyvesant Town and our sultry apartment in late summer. From August 24 to September 4, the high temperature was never less than ninety degrees and the nights were hardly cooler than the days. Still, returning was essential. School was starting, first grade for me and sixth grade for my brother, and there was no way our parents would allow us to miss a moment of our education.

P.S. 61, like the other schools in our neighborhood, remained as overcrowded as before, if not worse. The promised new schools were not yet built, so it was back to bizarre scheduling, packed classrooms, and sharing desks and workbooks that were supposed to teach the rudiments of reading and numbers. My friend who lived upstairs had moved away, her family wrenched apart by divorce and, I later learned, the dislocations of the blacklists.

Just as school began in the fall of 1953, Moskoff released his latest tally to newspapers and wire services: 150 under investigation, twenty-three who "admitted past party membership and have been allowed to retain their jobs after proving they left the party in good faith," fifteen awaiting trial, and 110 already dismissed, resigned, or retired in wake of the probes. What Moskoff did not mention to reporters was that the twenty-three teachers "allowed to retain their jobs" had earned that privilege by informing on their colleagues.

A year earlier, *Life* had featured the overcrowded conditions at my elementary school. Now its smaller, more conservative sister publication, *Time*, the country's leading national news magazine, championed the school administration that was doing so little to solve the overcrowding problem. The issue from October 19, 1953, featured a glowing profile of Superintendent William Jansen, with his portrait on the cover. The students were unruly, but he was expertly holding it all together. The profile made no mention of blacklists or teacher shortages, but it did focus on that newly sinister character that J. Edgar Hoover had recently spotted emerging from the shadows of collective anxiety: the teenager. Like Hoover, Jansen juggled the dual image of young people as fragile creatures needing protection from subversive ideas who were also volatile changelings who could easily be incited to riot.

The *Time* profile of Jansen began with a terrifying portrayal of the city's students. "Nobody warned me about a thing before I went to a near-slum district in Brooklyn," an anonymous young schoolteacher was quoted as saying. "I learned a lot of things about teaching that aren't in the books. In a high school like ours, you have a few tough ones and a few vicious ones in almost every class, and you have to watch them every second or they will take over your control of the others. If they do, you're lost." Luckily, the article continued, Jansen was at the helm, steering the ship of education through the rocky shoals of adolescence. Or so it seemed to the writers of *Time*.

That same month, Eleanor Roosevelt appeared as the mystery contestant on the popular television show *What's My Line?* Wearing decorative eye masks, four panelists posed a series of questions to the unseen celebrity, trying to guess the guest's identity and occupation. Two years earlier, poet and anthologist Louis Untermeyer, a panelist since the show's beginning, was abruptly fired when his name appeared in *Red Channels*, making him one of many artists and performers blacklisted for alleged communist associations based on acts like signing petitions or attending a peace conference. Now, actress Arlene Francis parodied House Un-American Activities Committee trials by asking the former First Lady, "Are you now or have you ever been . . . associated with politics?" The phrase, so familiar from broadcasts and newspaper accounts of congressional investigations, was being treated as though the blacklists didn't matter at all.

CHAPTER 23

When the Enemy Becomes a Joke

I was supposed to be asleep, but the people in the living room were roaring with laughter, keeping me awake. They were all listening to a record. It wasn't like the barbershop quartets and cowboy songs I adored at that time, or Burl Ives singing about the little white duck. It was someone talking, a man with a deep scary voice, but somehow the people in the living room thought it was very funny.

The album they were listening to remained on our shelves for many years, another skinny LP alongside the original cast album of *South Pacific* and the opera recordings my father liked. The cardboard sleeve that held the LP was white, with a few simple line drawings and the title: *The Investigator*. I didn't know it then, but my parents and their friends were listening to a political satire that mocked the bitter extremism of the day.

The target of the satire was Republican senator Joseph McCarthy, who had built his slimy career by asserting that the government was riddled with communist infiltrators and that he, and only he, could save the country. He and his close assistant, young New York attorney Roy Cohn, liked to accuse first and seek facts later, if ever. After Cohn's death from AIDS in 1986, playwright Tony Kushner made the dying lawyer a major character in his Pulitzer Prize–winning *Angels in America*. More recently, Cohn is cited as a mentor to the young Donald Trump, training his protégé in the art of suing everyone in sight while never admitting guilt for anything questionable.

In the early 1950s, Cohn had a different young protégé, G. David Shine, who had been drafted into the army as a private. When the army accused Cohn of using pressure to get undeserved promotions and other preferential treatment for Shine during his military service, Senator McCarthy claimed the accusations were retaliation against his investigations of alleged communist sympathizers in the military. He demanded his own hearings on the issue. It was a massive strategic error.

From April to June 1954, much of America was mesmerized by what were called the Army-McCarthy hearings, the first extended national event to be covered live on television. Not many people owned televisions, but some bought them just to witness the hearings. Others gathered outside appliance stores, watching television through the display windows. The hearings were covered on the radio, too, so many people became familiar with McCarthy's growling voice and hectoring manner.

While the Army-McCarthy hearings were going on, the Canadian Broadcast Network aired a radio play by Reuben Ship, a Hollywood writer who had returned to his native Canada after being blacklisted in California. In *The Investigator*, the nameless title character dies and goes to heaven, where he immediately starts questioning the loyalty of Socrates, Milton, Jefferson, and Voltaire. After assembling a committee of similarly relentless interrogators drawn from the Spanish Inquisition and the Salem witch trials, the Investigator decides to take on Saint Peter, and, finally, God—at which point he is removed from his committee and sent to hell, with all the wonderful shrieking and careening sound effects that radio programs do so well. It was not very subtle. If you had watched or listened to the Army-McCarthy hearings, as millions had, you would instantly recognize the lead actor's excellent imitation of McCarthy's distinctive voice.

The Investigator resonated with many listeners. The recording of the broadcast sold 100,000 copies in the United States, one of which ended up in my parents' living room. Rumor was that President Eisenhower owned the record, too, and played it for the amusement of some of the members of his cabinet. Eisenhower detested McCarthy and made a point of never actually saying the senator's name.

The Army-McCarthy hearings were the beginning of the end of well-publicized federal inquiries into alleged "un-American" activities, even if it took many years for blacklisted people to find work or, in some cases, regain their right to reenter the United States if they had fled to another country. The New York City teacher purges lasted at least until the late 1950s. In 1955, again at the urging of George Timone, the Board of Education reaffirmed that refusal to inform on other teachers was a justification for firing. It was not until 1959 that the New York State Supreme Court voided the board's policy. The change in political climate came too late to save my father's job, but as he listened to *The Investigator*, perhaps it began to seem like he and others on the blacklists might yet have the last laugh. I like to think so.

CHAPTER 24

Teaching Under the Radar

The search for "un-American" activities was often described as a broad program of national defense, but the impact was always personal. Being falsely accused, humiliated, robbed of your career, and forced to reinvent yourself was not as harsh as other punishments doled out by other political oppressors, past and present. But it was still punishment, cruel and capricious.

For at least five years, my father had been busy organizing parents, resisting the steamroller of the blacklists, and remembering the bitter events of the years before the war. But even as he fought to keep his job as a teacher and improve conditions in our grossly overcrowded schools, there was another current flowing through our house. It was the breezy life of glossy magazines and national advertisers, the world of slick photography and sophisticated tastemakers turning their energies to the glorification of consumption and domesticity. It was the world my mother now moved in, largely invisible to the rest of the family but emerging at peculiar times.

Haircuts, for example. My older brother got his hair cut at a dingy basement barbershop on Avenue B, south of Fourteenth Street. I would sometimes tag along and look at the grainy photos of nearly naked women in the girly magazines on a table near the door. For my haircuts, however, my mother preferred the children's salon at Best & Company, the upscale (and now defunct) department store on Fifth Avenue that had been catering to the carriage trade since the days when wealthy ladies in fact arrived at shops in horse-drawn carriages. I don't recall how I got there or why I was left alone to be alternately petted

Saul gives lesson plans to home economics teachers in his new career as *Seventeen*'s
consultant on consumer education. Credit: Collection of the author.

and threatened by the imperious stylist cutting my hair, but the unfamiliar luxury of the place left an indelible impression. The walls were
lined with framed pastel portraits of radiant children, all white and
mostly blond, very different from the magazine photos in my brother's
barbershop. The hairdresser dusted my neck with an impossibly soft
powder puff before sternly warning me not to move in any way. The
receptionist gave me a very special balloon on departure, transparent
except for three white stripes and the words "Best & Company" written across the center. Then my mother would appear to take me out
for ice cream if she had time or rush me back home in a taxi if she did
not. Apparently, she wanted to introduce me to a higher level of commerce than the bodegas on the other side of Fourteenth Street.

Baby pictures were another index of change. There are lovely matte
portraits of my older brother Stephen and of me as babies, done by
anonymous photographers whose work was included as a bonus for diaper service subscribers. My parents always called these "the diaper
service pictures," a demeaning name for high-quality work. When my
brother Jonathan arrived in 1953, on the last day of October, we traded
the deckle-edged diaper service portraits for journalistic status.

Arthur Rothstein, famed for his Dust Bowl photographs for the Farm Services Administration during the Great Depression, now lived nearby in Peter Cooper Village and was my mother's friend and colleague at *Look* magazine. Shortly after Jonathan was born, Arthur came to our apartment to take a family portrait. I have the glossies and the contact sheets, my father and older brother in suits and bow ties, me in a crisply ironed dress, and my mother seated in our Colonial reproduction rocking chair and holding in her arms the barely visible new baby. Behind us is the fireplace wall copied from the Metropolitan's American Wing. These are nice photos, though not as focused on the new baby as the diaper service portraits. They represent a higher level of sophistication.

New books were entering the house, too. Hardbound catalogs from the Museum of Modern Art and best-selling novels joined my father's beloved classics on the shelves. To me, the most wonderful was a magic volume called *The Flair Annual for 1953*, an oversized book with a striking red-and-gold binding and an array of foldout, pop-up, die-cut pages that enchanted me long before I learned they had been designed by surrealist artist Salvador Dalí. Federico Pallavicini was the art director of *Flair*, another Cowles publication that shared office space with *Look*, and the title page of our copy of *Flair Annual* was embellished with his tiny watercolor painting of an ornate frame enclosing the words "I Love Sylvia."

The title of the book was misleading, since this was the only annual for *Flair*, a beautiful but crushingly expensive magazine published for less than a year, ending in January 1951. My mother worked on *Flair* as well as on *Look* and spent her days in the glass-and-steel aerie of Cowles Publications in Midtown Manhattan. She came home with stories of Fleur Cowles, editor of *Flair* and, not coincidentally, wife of publisher Gardner Cowles. My mother hired young Andy Warhol to illustrate her food stories, went on photo shoots with celebrated photojournalists, interviewed celebrities at the Palm Court of the Plaza Hotel, and moved in a glamorous world her husband and children barely knew.

Sylvia was proud of Saul's principles and shared his liberal politics, but she was also aware that her job paid a good deal more than he had earned as a teacher. By the time the new baby arrived, she felt it was time to help him find a less fraught and better-paid career. And she had one in mind. After a marital conversation I cannot even imagine, my father took his skill at teaching and writing lesson plans, combined them with native intelligence and an affable nature, and made an appointment with the editor in chief of *Seventeen* magazine, the self-proclaimed Bible of the teenage girl. Sylvia had worked at *Seventeen* before moving to *Look* and still had friends there, including the editor in chief. Barred from teaching English to budding boy mechanics, Saul would pivot to educating their sisters.

In an era when young women often married before they were twenty, *Seventeen* supplemented its coverage of fashion and dating with stories on cooking, furniture buying, and other aspects of starting a home. Although he had no domestic skills of any kind, my father offered himself to the editor as an advisor to teachers of what was then called home economics. He would develop a consumer education curriculum that would be distributed for free by the magazine, a form of public relations designed to build readership and please advertisers. He would lead classes on field trips to the supermarket to train the students to be smart shoppers. He would make guest appearances in their classrooms. And always, everywhere, he would remind his students that they could learn more about the products he used in his demonstrations by reading about them in *Seventeen*.

The pitch worked, and so did the newly reinvented self. He had no tenure and no union, but year after year his contract was renewed as a full-time "educational consultant," earning at least twice what he would have made as a teacher. For the next fifteen years, Saul worked for *Seventeen* and then an equal time for *Good Housekeeping*, where consumer information was a vital part of the magazine's Good Housekeeping Institute, an in-house rival to the product-testing giant, Consumer Reports. He attended teacher conventions and educational conferences, handing out lesson plan packets and convincing teachers and administrators to incorporate his sessions on comparison shopping and nutrition into their more traditional classes in how to make white sauce or sew an apron. He went to trade shows to pick up tips on new household products. He subscribed to *Supermarket News* and *Chain Store Age*, and if he didn't quite lose himself in their pages the way he did when reading Tolstoy or Dante, he paid enough attention to keep up with trends he could then pass on to his audiences. This career lasted far longer than his teaching days and was far freer of controversy. And yet, if anyone had been interested, they might have thought he was still spreading subversive ideas.

It was an unlikely career in many ways, but its most striking feature, at least in hindsight, was that nobody seemed to worry that this roving ambassador of consumer education might be using his job as a way of introducing dangerous precepts to susceptible young minds. No one thought he was subverting the free enterprise system or the "American Way of Life" by encouraging teenage girls to be educated consumers, wise to the ways of the companies that vied for their attention and their future household budgets. Not the school district supervisors who invited him into their schools or the teachers around the country who happily used his lesson plans. Not the magazine publishers who hired him or the advertisers who indirectly paid his salary. Not the teenage girls who brought their notebooks on field trips to explore the aisles of local supermarkets and took home recipes for feeding a family on a budget. And certainly not the investigators and informers who had hounded him out of the New York City schools. Like the blacklisted artists who found new careers writing picture books or recording songs for children, Saul had slipped under the radar of the professional red hunters.

In 1956, my mother finally found her center-entry colonial, the house of her dreams. That fall, we moved from Manhattan to New Rochelle. When I entered fourth grade at a spacious, newly built school, I was amazed to encounter novelties like music classes, art, and gym. Even more surprising, every single student in my new school spoke English. My older brother had been admitted to the academic elite at New York City's Stuyvesant High School, but now he was in a vast suburban high school where advanced placement classes coexisted with fraternities and sororities, vocational classes, a football field, and traditions and assumptions very different from those he had known before.

My father, too, found himself in a new world, with much to learn. Our neighbors now had sailboats and gardens, but few showed any interest in the political activism that had been so big a part of his life. He learned to breed dahlias and avoid discussing current events.

Work, too, was a plunge into a very different world, with its own adjustments. Saul found his new career worthwhile, but he was well aware of how far he had come from introducing students to a love of literature or just the basics of reading. Now he spent his days promoting new creations with canned tuna. I have many photographs of my father at work, the only man in a room full of home economics teachers dressed in beautifully tailored dresses and suits they had made themselves, sometimes with matching hats and purses crafted from the leftover fabric. He went to supermarket conventions and houseware shows in giant exposition halls where he posed for photos next to fading movie stars selling their former celebrity to gadget manufacturers. He studied the basics of upholstery so he could help sewing teachers plan lessons that went beyond dressmaking.

At his own booth, he was photographed standing solemnly before colorful charts retelling the latest nutritional guidelines, ready to hand out lesson plans to all comers. He invented a cartoon sidekick, Sunny Seven, to help explain the Seven Basic Food Groups, and then retired his buddy when the Department of Agriculture decided to consolidate its nutrition advice to a Basic Four, and then a wheel, and then a food pyramid. He created a weeklong curriculum around the single topic of "Read the Label."

If one of the many regional teachers' conferences Saul attended became too tedious, he would play reverse hooky by going back to school. He would find the nearest college and locate the theater department. There he would ask any available faculty if there were any good plays on campus. Sometimes he would also take them out to lunch at whatever restaurant they recommended. After all, his expense account covered research into the history of fashion, and he decided that included theatrical costumes. In time, he collaborated with one of his new theater department friends on a course packet on dress in the age of Shakespeare that entered the collection of the Folger Shakespeare Library in Washington, D.C.

Mostly, though, he stuck to the convention halls and to his public school teachers of home economics. However unexpected my father found his new life to be, he sincerely liked the teachers and state supervisors with whom he worked. He believed, possibly more than he ever had as an English teacher, that he was helping shape the citizens of the future. He also got to see the country, which he enjoyed. Long hours in airplanes and hotel rooms left him plenty of time to read the classic nineteenth-century novels that were his lifelong passion. There were conflicts and office politics, I'm sure, but nothing at the level of intimidation he had already endured.

As I consider the last thirty years of my father's life, I wonder what happened to that eager idealist who had volunteered to supervise the school newspaper or organize the paper drive. He was still ready to sign a petition against religion in public education, join a march against the Vietnam War, or write a letter to the newspaper shaming those who resisted school integration. He relished the downfall of Joseph McCarthy. But he had lost his youthful sense that he lived in a nation of selfless patriots, and his days of active organizing were over. Whatever his later triumphs, he had been beaten by the system and had retreated in quiet cynicism. When the Teachers Union disbanded in 1964, driven to extinction by continuing political pressure, my father didn't mention it.

In a jumbled box of family snapshots very different from the secret accordion file, I found pictures of my father during his years with *Seventeen* and *Good Housekeeping*. These photos are often just as mysterious as the records of his investigation, though in different ways. What is he doing with that rag doll that he holds in the air like a trophy? Why is his head poking out of a giant bottle of molasses? How is magician David Copperfield levitating my father? But what really separates these later photos from the earlier ones is the transformation of the solemn young man who picketed in Albany and led parents to crowded meetings of the city Board of Estimate. The older Saul, submitting himself to all sorts of promotional nonsense, is always smiling.

Saul was working for *Good Housekeeping* in December 1981 when the president of City College held a reception for the survivors of the blacklists, with special attention to the ten teachers who had sued the Board of Education and been reinstated two months earlier, thirty years after their firing. My father attended. At the time, he only said that he had been at a City College reunion and had met up with some fellow former teachers. He would not have mentioned it at all, I think, but he wanted to tell me that at this gathering he had reconnected with the father of my earliest friend, the little girl upstairs. She was now a professor at the University of Illinois, the same state where I now lived. He had also bumped into Sam Wallach, whose daughter Joan Wallach Scott had been a member of the history department at Northwestern before she left for the University of North Carolina and Brown University, later joining the Institute for Advanced Study in Princeton, New Jersey. He wondered if we had known each other in Evanston, though I am sorry to report we did not.

Richard Flacks, son of the beloved elementary school teacher and *Teachers News* editor who accompanied my father to Saul Moskoff's office, also became a professor. So did Lewis Siegelbaum, son of the teacher-turned-computer salesman. Was there any significance to this lineup of college professors, the children of blacklisted teachers? We were not being groomed for revenge, but we all came from families that put a very high value on education.

Toward the end of his life, my father once remarked to me that he should have stayed in teaching. "I would have a pension," he said, comparing himself to the teachers who had gone to court and were vindicated decades later. Given how small those pensions were, I think he was also regretting his failure to take a more visible stand, to go through the difficult but brave route of public trial rather than resigning.

Sometimes, after some particularly stunning extravagance on my mother's part, he would turn to me in resignation and ask, "What happened to that communist I married?" I had thought it was a figure of speech, a rueful exaggeration of how much their lives had changed since their flat-broke days as newlyweds. Looking back, I realize it is possible my father was at some time a member of the Communist Party, and my mother as well. It is also entirely possible they were not, and he was referring to her long-ago rhetoric and not any actual political activity. I'll never know for sure, any more than I will know the youthful actions and later fates of most of the other teachers harried out of the classroom in the 1950s.

In the end, I return to the question of why the anti-communist forces were so afraid. My father was typical of the blacklisted teachers, struggling to retain—and impart—democratic principles in a society that seemed increasingly focused on fear, repression, and devotion to unchecked capitalism, with all the inequality that fostered. Even if he had wanted to undermine the government of the United States, which I in no way believe, his classroom would have been a very small and wobbly platform from which to do so. He encouraged teenagers to read books, write for student publications, and collect wastepaper and scrap metal during World War II. His students seemed to like him. They fashioned wooden toys for his new baby during their shop classes and appreciated the way he made their classes in the Annex feel like they were still connected to their school. They played punchball with him. The verifiable record shows he was also a Boy Scout leader, though possibly more likely to lead expeditions to the Metropolitan Museum than into the woods. He was an energetic president of the local PTA who worked to relieve overcrowding at his children's elementary school and a campaigner for better pay for teachers and safer schools for students. He was also an irrepressible do-gooder who donated $250 a year to the Red Cross when that represented 5 percent of his pretax salary.

Perhaps that made him a subversive. If, like Senator Joseph McCarthy and the radio agitator Father Coughlin, you believe that a subversive is anyone who supports labor unions and opposes racism, then you are ready to convict. If you operate on the assumption that your success depends on the failure of everybody else, then ending the career of one teacher, or a hundred, or a thousand was a triumph. If you think any reader of a liberal magazine is a single-minded follower of Moscow, or if you are ready to give full credit to informants and teachers threatened with dismissal if they didn't "name names," then it becomes possible to believe the schools of New York were swarming with communist agents dedicated to overthrowing the American government by seducing impressionable young people with their twisted views.

If, like my father, you suspect the accusations against him were acts of revenge—first for his attempts to expose financial misdeeds and pro-fascist activities before World War II and later for his battle with school officials about the need for new buildings to relieve overcrowded schools—well, that's another story.

The schoolhouse has always been a contested space, a battlefield for proxy wars of class, religion, race, gender, and other issues polarizing the adult world. People in power, and particularly people anxious about losing that power, have always resisted efforts to expand the borders of what is taught, who can teach it, and who should be allowed to learn. Often, the stated rationale is that they are protecting children, as though they could seal the young in a conflict-proof vacuum safely located somewhere in a mythic better past. The reality is that whatever the details of the current battle, teachers are often the first casualties, and children are always caught in the crossfire.

CHAPTER 25

The Past Is Always Present

The people most active in the New York City teacher purges were honored and rewarded for their work. William Jansen remained as the well-paid superintendent of schools until his retirement in 1958, and he was an honored man to the end of his life. In 1959, Saul Moskoff left the Board of Education and returned to the Office of the Corporation Counsel. Soon after, he was appointed a judge to the Queens County Family Court, a position he held until he reached mandatory retirement age in 1981. Arthur Levitt, the Board of Education president who served as trial examiner for teachers who refused to go quietly by resigning or retiring, became New York State comptroller in 1955, a post he held until 1970. Daniel Scannell, an assistant prosecutor, went on to be executive director of the Metropolitan Transit Authority.

The special investigations unit of the New York City Police Department moved seamlessly from investigating liberal teachers and other citizens for possible communist ties to investigating the countercultural agents of the 1960s: hippies, anarchists, anti-war protesters, student radicals, and anyone working for racial justice. It is entirely likely that both the police and the FBI are conducting similar surveillance right now, greatly enhanced by the more powerful tools of the Internet age but still too often looking in the wrong direction. In 2020, as white supremacist militias and far-right conspiracy mongers grew in power, encouraging the mob that would storm the Capitol on January 6, 2021, the FBI was ordered yet again to ignore them and instead search for groups and individuals protesting racism and repression. The "premature anti-fascists" of the 1930s are now reviled as "antifa," short for anti-fascist, and the exaggerated fear of liberalism and the blithe tolerance of violent right-wing organizations remain.

Repressive attacks on students, teachers, and the entire enterprise of public education also continue, energized and legitimized by the successes of the Trump administration and its admirers. In 2016, students in Detroit, Michigan, filed a class action lawsuit arguing that their dismal public schools deprived them of access to literacy and thus violated their rights to citizenship under the Fourteenth Amendment; in 2018, a judge rejected their suit, ruling that literacy was not a fundamental right. On appeal, the Sixth Circuit Court of Appeals overturned that ruling, but by a divided decision that will very probably be appealed again. In the hearts of too many people, the nineteenth-century constitutional amendments and statutes meant to ensure equal rights are open to question or even repeal. As I write in 2025, Ron DeSantis governs Florida on a platform designed to drag education back to the Jim Crow era, weaken voting rights, and remove women's control of their own bodies.

The temptation to get rid of a troublemaking teacher by calling him or her a political seducer is equally hard to squash. In the spring of 2017, a Brooklyn principal, Jill Bloomberg, was visited by the New York City Department of Education's Office of Special Investigations. According to the *New York Times* report on May 5, "The representative told Ms. Bloomberg that she could not tell her the nature of any allegations, nor who had made them." When Bloomberg sued, her lawyer was told that the investigation was triggered by accusations that she belonged to the Progressive Labor Party, a communist organization, and that she and two other teachers in the school were accused of recruiting students to the party and inviting them to attend marches.

Many of her supporters believed that Bloomberg was really being attacked for her outspoken criticism of the Board of Education and her advocacy for Black and Latinx students who were forced to endure crumbling schools and unequal access to resources. Almost six months later, after denying that the investigation was a violation of the principal's civil rights, the Office of Special Investigations declared that it had been unable to substantiate the charge that Bloomberg had been recruiting students for the Progressive Labor Party. Without naming the original complainant, the OSI report noted that the person had failed to provide any evidence to support the accusation.

Attacks on teachers and efforts to straightjacket education continue. In 2024, at least twenty states had laws restricting teachers from discussing so-called divisive concepts in their classrooms, from race and slavery to the long and changing history of gender identity. Also in 2024, the Oklahoma State superintendent of public instruction required all teachers to incorporate the Bible and the Ten Commandments in their curriculum, a clear violation of the separation of church and state and a continuation of earlier efforts to mandate Christianity in public education.

Sometimes the language of contemporary attacks on teachers seems a direct copy of 1950s rhetoric. On September 17, 2020, when President Trump called protests against police brutality "left-wing rioting and mayhem . . . the direct result of decades of left-wing indoctrination in our schools," it was impossible not to hear the echo of that earlier time when other politicians and self-proclaimed moral authorities worked with great success to demonize liberal teachers and force them out of schools. Then, too, student protests were blamed on "left-wing indoctrination." Then and now, the needs of students and the rights of teachers were sacrificed to a self-serving vision of ideological purity that had nothing to do with education.

In both eras, curriculum battles and book bans reflect a deeply dangerous assumption that politicians and government agents can pick and choose the "truths" they like and then impose them on the public. Today, the bogus claim is that children will be traumatized by reading about past injustices or seduced into gender fluidity by learning about the existence of people who don't fully identify with the gender they were assigned at birth. The anguish of those whose history is distorted or ignored by these false narratives does not matter, and neither does the damage to the schools and libraries that lose their cherished role as repositories of ideas. Nor do the courts escape the damage they sometimes permit. In the age of blacklists, judges sometimes bent the law to serve the purpose of zealots and opportunists, and the structure of rights—including the right to education—was shaken almost to the breaking point. Too many of the same distortions are twisting jurisprudence today.

There have always been blacklists, just as there have always been banned books, but calling such horrors "cyclical" misses an important element. Each return to repression is informed and empowered by the one before, and each cycle extends the reach of the ones that preceded it. The forced closure of socialist schools and radical publishing houses in the 1920s led to the more extensive blacklisting of public school teachers in the 1950s, which paved the way for the even broader bans and strictures on education today.

In some important respects, the school crackdowns of today are worse than earlier attempts to force education to fit narrow ideological norms. Blacklisted teachers of the 1950s were fired, but they were not threatened with prison if they dared to mention forbidden words. Children were not callously exposed to random shootings, betrayed by politicians too ready to side with Second Amendment extremists rather than stop the carnage. But the forces that roil our current classrooms have their roots in the past, in buried passions and hate-filled agendas that have reemerged to claim the center stage in what was and remains a melodrama of posturing politics.

The teachers driven out of their classrooms by the blacklists of the 1950s lost their jobs and often their idealism, but the real losers were the students who never got to hear the varied perspectives those teachers might have offered. Once again, we are faced with self-appointed arbiters who seek to prevent young people from learning about the real diversity of the world they inhabit, restricting their knowledge in ways that will only narrow their futures and weaken the fabric of society. As we strive to rebuild democracy in a better, broader, more equitable way, we must remember the past. We must make sure the schoolhouse door remains open to all teachers, all students, and all ideas. We must call out demagogues as the unscrupulous self-promoters they are. And we must reject the politics of fear.

Acknowledgments

When I realized that my early memories and mysterious family relics were part of a much larger saga, I knew I would need a great deal of help to fill in the story. Librarians and archivists at the Tamiment Library and Robert F. Wagner Labor Archives at New York University, the Oral History Archives at Columbia University, Special Collections at Northwestern University, the Seeley G. Mudd Manuscript Library at Princeton University, the Harry Ransom Center at the University of Texas, and Special Collection at University of Detroit Mercy all graciously helped me locate and use historical material related to the New York City teacher blacklists. Archivists at the New York City Municipal Archives patiently provided access to the voluminous holdings of the New York City Board of Education Anti-communist Investigation Records and related archives. Special thanks go to David Ment, who has an encyclopedic knowledge of this collection. The archivists and curators at the Huntington Library in San Marino, California, were unfailingly helpful; I am particularly grateful to Diann Benti, who energetically carved a path for me through uncataloged boxes of anti-communist literature. Chris Hagedorn, publisher of Hagedorn Communications, let me pore over bound volumes of *Town & Village*, the weekly newspaper that has documented daily life in Stuyvesant Town and Peter Cooper Village from the early days of these two adjacent Manhattan housing projects; it was there I first learned of the central role my father had played in the yearslong struggle to relieve school overcrowding for those instant cities so very full of little children.

Other people whose parents had been forced out of teaching jobs during the blacklist years generously shared their memories and family records. Lisa Harbatkin, whose unsuccessful lawsuit to gain unrestricted access to the Board of Education Anti-Communist Archives first alerted me to the very existence of this hidden material, later guided me to several other important sources she is using for her own research and writing. Richard Flacks, whose father David Flacks accompanied mine to his interrogations, spoke with me at length and gave me access to records of his parents' experience as courageous reformers and embattled teachers. Lewis Siegelbaum shared both his writings and his memories of his father's truncated career as a teacher. Joan Wallach Scott, historian and outspoken child of the blacklist and its legacy, has provided extraordinary support and encouragement as well as personal information and necessary corrections. Our new friendship was one of the unexpected rewards of delving into the dark days of teacher suppression.

I am very grateful to historians and writers extraordinaire Kevin Boyle and Richard White for their incisive and constructive comments on earlier drafts. Investigative journalist Hella Winston generously shared her own research into the Board of Education anti-communist efforts. Suzie Tibor provided crucial help in gathering illustrations and permissions under a challenging deadline, as did United Federation of Teachers archivist Tom Dickson. Stephanie Steiker made many helpful suggestions. Editor Peggy Solic's enthusiastic support brought this book to Rutgers University Press, for which many thanks. A courtesy appointment in the History Department at Northwestern University has given me a home from which to conduct my research and writing; it has been a great boon.

My family heard me talk about this project for far longer than any of us expected. To my brothers, Stephen Schur and Jonathan Schur, I owe thanks for their willingness to let me explore our family history and make it public. My uncle Philip Zipser, who died in 2024 at the age of one hundred and three, shared memories of life in the 1930s and 1940s, including the passionate politics of New York City college students and his vivid memories of my father's despair at losing his job in 1953. My children, Jeremy Smith and Lucia Smith, were early readers and kind but unsparing critics. As ever, my deepest gratitude is to my husband, Carl Smith, the best companion in research and in life anyone could hope to have. I cannot thank him enough.

Note on Sources

The New York City school purges have faded from memory, but their records remain. There are rich troves of information about blacklists, purges, and anti-liberal movements in the New York City Schools. The Robert F. Wagner Labor Archives at New York University contain extensive files on conflicts at Gompers High School; these archives cite my father and other teachers, subsequently ousted, whose names are familiar to me for reasons I never understood when I heard them as a child. Many more documents relating to organized efforts to rid the schools of allegedly subversive teachers are in the Board of Education Records at the New York City Municipal Archives, both in the special category of anti-communist records and in the individual papers of William Jansen and Saul Moskoff. The 1963 *Reminiscences of William Jansen* are part of the Columbia University Oral History Archives. Investigation files of the Rapp-Coudert Committee are held by the New York State Archives in Albany; copies are available at the Tamiment Library at New York University. Records of the Teachers Union are housed at Cornell University and in the Robert F. Wagner Labor Archives at New York University. Bound copies of *Town & Village* are at the company offices of Hagedorn Communications in New Rochelle, New York; I am deeply grateful to Chris Hagedorn for granting me access.

Among the many accounts published in the 1950s concerning blacklists and communist threats, several books stand out. *School of Darkness* is the 1955 confessional memoir by Bella Dodd, the lawyer and legislative director of the Teachers Union who became an enthusiastic informer after being reconverted from communism to Catholicism by the staunchly anti-communist television evangelist Bishop Fulton Sheen. *False Witness*, Harvey Matusow's 1955 tell-all account of his profitable career as a paid informer, includes vivid descriptions of the places that served as hearing rooms and interrogation chambers. Neither book is factually reliable, but both evoke the atmosphere of the times. Hyman Lumer's *The Professional Informer*, also from 1955, is less sensational but provides many details of the business of side of turning in suspected subversives. *This Happened in Pasadena* is David Hulburd's 1951 play-by-play account of the ouster of Superintendent Willard Goslin, archenemy of the California school conservatives. Martin Lawrence's *Faceless Informers and Our Schools*, a series of articles first published in the *Denver Post* and then republished as a twenty-eight-page booklet in 1954, is another contemporaneous account of the school blacklists, including a chapter on the New York City school investigations.

Several more recent books discuss the New York school purges, often as part of a much larger narrative of McCarthyism and political conflicts in education. Clarence Taylor's *Reds at the Blackboard: Communism, Civil Rights, and the New York City Teachers Union*; Andrew Hartman's *Education and the Cold War: The Battle for the American School*; Andrew Feffer's *Bad Faith: Teachers, Liberalism, and the Origins of McCarthyism*; Marjorie Heins's *Priests of Our Democracy: The Supreme Court, Academic Freedom, and the Anti-Communist Purge*; and Ellen Schrecker's *Many Are the Crimes: McCarthyism in America* all detail the battles that swirled around schools. Beverly Gage's masterful *G-Man: J. Edgar Hoover and the Making of the American Century* contains many revelations of the clandestine anti-radical investigations of the FBI and Hoover's willingness to share his files with state and local officials in charge of education in the 1950s. Cathleen Thom and Patrick Jung's "The Responsibilities Program of the FBI, 1951–1955" (*The Historian*, Winter 1997) details the ways Hoover's sharing became an instrument of harassment, especially in education. Jo-Anne Brown's "'A Is for Atom, B Is for Bomb': Civil Defense in American Public Education, 1948–1963," in the June 1988 issue of *Journal of American History*, confirmed and amplified my childhood memories of dog tags and air raid drills. Paul D. Tillett's unpublished research for *The Social Costs of the Loyalty Programs*, now at the Seeley G. Mudd Manuscript Library at Princeton University, helped me see the reach of anti-communist programs in neighboring states.

The purge of New York City teachers was part of a much longer national movement to make America "safe" from liberals. *Revolutionary Radicalism: Its History, Purpose and Tactics with an Exposition and Discussion of the Steps Being Taken and Required to Curb It, Being the Report of the Joint Legislative Committee Investigating Seditious Activities,* published in 1920 in four fat volumes, details the New York State Legislature's earliest response to the perceived communist threat, as compiled by the Lusk commission. The Marie Koenig Collection at the Huntington Library in San Marino, California, unfortunately unavailable to researchers at this time, contains a trove of midcentury anti-communist ephemera among its holdings, much of it luridly illustrated, including publications specifically about the need to rid the New York City schools of progressive thinkers. Michelle Nickerson's *Mothers of Conservatism: Women and the Postwar Right* details the background and context of this collection, which also contains defenses of the New York teachers from as far away as Denver and London. Steven Ross's *Hitler in Los Angeles: How Jews Foiled Nazi Plots against Hollywood and America* is an invaluable guide to German influences on American politics in the years before World War II. Rachel Maddow's *Prequel: An American Fight against Fascism* also investigates that fraught period of fascist power in the United States.

Once again, I wish to thank the other children of blacklisted teachers who generously shared their family records and their memories. I have already cited Richard Flacks, Lisa Harbatkin, Joan Wallach Scott, and Lewis Siegelbaum. Several other firsthand accounts went dark when the invaluable website Dreamers and Fighters: The NYC Teacher Purges was taken down, but there is hope that it will soon be restored.

Much of my material is taken from family records and conversations. Decades of photographs and souvenirs show my father's life as student, teacher, soldier, PTA president, whistleblower, community "man of the year," blacklist victim, and, finally and most improbably, as an outcast who found a new way to teach by shaping curriculum for home economics teachers across the country. Memory is always unreliable, especially after so much time, but I have tried my best to verify and document what I recall.

.

Index

About the Author

JANE S. SMITH is a prizewinning author of fiction and nonfiction, including *Patenting the Sun: Polio and the Salk Vaccine*, *The Garden of Invention: Luther Burbank and the Business of Breeding Plants*, and *Fool's Gold*, a comic novel. She received her PhD from Yale University and has taught at Northwestern University on topics ranging from modern fiction to the history of public health. She lives in Chicago, where she works in a very small room with a very large window. Visit her at www.janessmith.com.